A CLIMBING GUIDE

ecuador
A CLIMBING GUIDE

Yossi Brain

THE
MOUNTAINEERS

Published by
The Mountaineers Books
1001 SW Klickitat Way, Suite 201
Seattle, WA 98134

Published simultaneously in Great Britain by Cordee, 3a DeMontfort Street, Leicester, England, LE1 7HD

Manufactured in the United States of America

Project Editor: Christine Ummel Hosler
Editor: Paula Thurman
Fact checkers: Jean Brown of Quito, Ecuador, and Peter Heck of Arizona State University
Maps by Aldo Mercado
All photographs by Yossi Brain
Topos by Janice Pacheco
Topos scanned by Eric Lawrie
Original map and topo design by Carmen Julia Arze
Cover design by Peggy Egerdahl
Book layout by Amy Winchester
Book design by Ani Rucki
Cover photograph: *Cotopaxi from Sincholagua*
Frontispiece: *Cumbre Nor-Oriental Antisana*

Library of Congress Cataloging-in-Publication Data
Brain, Yossi, 1967-1999
    Ecuador : a climbing guide / Yossi Brain.— 1st ed.
      p.   cm.
    Includes bibliographical references (p.) and index.
    ISBN 0-89886-729-0
    1. Mountaineering—Ecuador—Guidebooks. 2. Ecuador—Guidebooks.
I. Title.
GV199.44.E2 B72 2000
796.52'2'09866—dc21

                                       00-008962
                                       CIP

Contents

Acknowledgments 8
Introduction 9

CHAPTER 1 the mountains 12

CHAPTER 2 preparations 34

CHAPTER 3 chiles 55

CHAPTER 4 cotacachi 60

CHAPTER 5 mojanda 65
    Fuya Fuya 65
    Cerro Negro 67

CHAPTER 6 guagua pichincha 70

CHAPTER 7 ilinizas 74
    Iliniza Norte 77
    Iliniza Sur 79

CHAPTER 8 carihuairazo 84
    Cumbre Máxima 85

CHAPTER 9 chimborazo 89
    Cumbre Whymper 90
    Cumbre Politécnica 94
    Cumbre Nicolás Martínez 94
    Traverses 95

CHAPTER 10 **imbabura** 96

CHAPTER 11 **cayambe** 99
    Cumbre Máxima 103
    Pico Nor-Este 107

CHAPTER 12 **sara urcu** 108

CHAPTER 13 **antisana** 112
    Cumbre Máxima 115
    Cumbre Nor-Oriental 118
    Cumbre Oriental 120
    Pico Sur 122
    Traverse 124

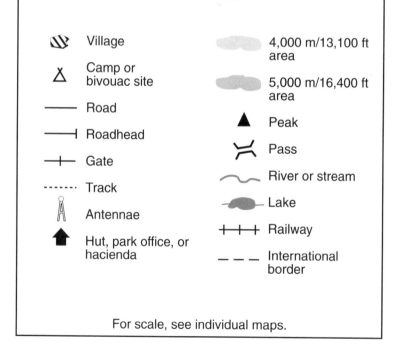

MAP KEY

ᗺ	Village			4,000 m/13,100 ft area
△	Camp or bivouac site			5,000 m/16,400 ft area
——	Road	▲		Peak
——⊣	Roadhead	⋈		Pass
——+—	Gate	∼		River or stream
------	Track	◼		Lake
⚊	Antennae	+++		Railway
⬆	Hut, park office, or hacienda	− − −		International border

For scale, see individual maps.

CHAPTER 14 sincholagua 125

CHAPTER 15 rumiñahui 131
Rumiñahui Central and Rumiñahui Norte 131
Rumiñahui Sur 134

CHAPTER 16 cotopaxi 136

CHAPTER 17 quilindaña 141

CHAPTER 18 hermoso 144

CHAPTER 19 tungurahua 150

CHAPTER 20 el altar 155
Southern El Altar Peaks 161
Obispo 161
Monja Grande 164
Monja Chica 164
Northern El Altar Peaks 167
Canónigo 167
The Frailes 167

CHAPTER 21 sangay 169

Appendix A: Medical Kit 178
Appendix B: Equipment 180
Appendix C: Further Reading 184
Index 187

Acknowledgments

Thanks to the following climbers with whom I have climbed routes in Ecuador for the first time: Allen Abramson (U.K.), Anne Marthiensen, Ulli Schatz (Germany), Jon Doran, Damaris Carlisle, Sean Delahunty (U.K.), Matheus (Belgium) and Christian, Marina, and Frederique (France), Ray Marx and Tim "Lightweight" Tadder (U.S.), Megs Crabtree (U.K.), and John Zazzara (U.S.).

For miscellaneous help, thanks to the following people: Chris Adye for a lot of information a long time ago, Dr. John Triplett for letting me see his copy of *The Fool's Guide,* Jean Brown, David Gayton, Javier Herrera, and Pattie Serrano at Safari, Gerry Arcari at Terra Nova and then Rab, Pete Stewart at Cotswold, Simon Morley at STA Travel, Dr. Minard "Pete" Hall, Escuela Politécnica Nacional, Sheila Corwin, South American Explorers' Club Quito, Lindsay Griffin, Jaime Avila, Mario Vásconez, Edison Oña, Gabriel Llano, Ecuadorian consul in La Paz Xavier Bustamante, Fernando Cobo, and Dr. Bernard Francou, Orstom.

Thanks to the following librarians for their help in locating random bits and pieces of information: Margaret Ecclestone, Alpine Club Library, London; Elsa Claret-Tournier, Bibliotheque d'Ecôle National de Ski et Alpinisme, Chamonix; and Josep Paytubi, Servei General d'Informació de Muntanya, Sabadell.

Special thanks for hospitality in Ecuador to Damaris Carlisle and Sean Delahunty (and for taking Betty to the limit), Ray Marx, and Nina Binder; Tim Tadder for jeep use and abuse; and Jean Brown for sharing some of her encyclopedic knowledge of Ecuador plus some good lifts to some out-of-the-way places.

Introduction

Outrageously easy access to high mountains makes Ecuador an excellent place to get some experience of high-altitude mountaineering. Using public transport from the capital city of Quito, you can arrive at the base of eight of the country's Big Ten mountains the same day and summit the next day—as long as you are acclimatized and conditions are fine. This means that once you are acclimatized, you can get a lot done in a short time. Ecuador has a well-deserved reputation for a good selection of easy routes, but it also offers technically hard routes and, surprisingly, new route possibilities.

Ecuador is the second smallest South American republic. At 272,045 km²/106,268 sq mi (including the Galápagos Islands), it is similar in size to Oregon, 10 percent bigger than Great Britain, or half the size of France or Spain. Yet it is one of the most diverse countries in the world in terms of geography, natural beauty, culture, and people. There are eleven million Ecuadorians: 40 percent are Indian and speak the traditional language, Quichua; 40 percent are mixed Spanish-Indian; 10 percent are white; 5 percent are black; and 5 percent are other heritages. Almost half the population lives in the high central valleys called the Sierra, with altitude varying from 1,800 m/5,900 ft to 3,000 m/9,800 ft.

Ecuador has the highest density of population in South America and the highest rate of literacy—compulsory schooling was introduced in Ecuador before it was made mandatory in Great Britain. Oil, bananas, shrimp, tourism, roses, cocoa, and coffee are the country's main sources of income, in that order.

Politically, economically, and geologically Ecuador is one of the most unstable countries in South America. Revolutions, currency devaluations, earthquakes, and volcanic eruptions are not uncommon and are nothing new. Alfred Simson, in *Travels in the Wilds of Ecuador* (1886), commented on the history of Ecuador as "a constant repetition of rebellion among the troops and people, with consequent numberless and complicated revolutions and changes of Presidents, Supreme Chiefs,

Carihuairazo's summit ridge and Tungurahua

Provisional Commissioners, and Dictators." However, beyond the inconvenience of general strikes, not knowing how much your money is worth, electricity outages and water shortages following earthquakes, and volcano alerts of varying degrees of seriousness, there is nothing to stop you from having a good time and getting the routes in.

A NOTE ABOUT SAFETY

Safety is an important concern in all outdoor activities. No guidebook can alert you to every hazard or anticipate the limitations of every reader. Therefore, the descriptions of roads, trails, routes, and natural features in this book are not representations that a particular place or excursion will be safe for your party. When you follow any of the routes described in this book, you assume responsibility for your own safety. Under normal conditions, such excursions require the usual attention to traffic, road and trail conditions, weather, terrain, the capabilities of your party, and other factors. Keeping informed on current conditions and exercising common sense are the keys to a safe, enjoyable outing.

Political conditions may add to the risks of travel in South America in ways that this book cannot predict. When you travel, you assume this risk, and should keep informed of political developments that may make safe travel difficult or impossible.

The Mountaineers Books

CHAPTER 1

the mountains

The mountains are beautiful but above all exotic. On the same climb

one can fight tropical vegetation, stroll up a glacier, and look down

the crater of a live volcano.

Michael Koerner
The Fool's Climbing Guide to Ecuador and Peru (1976)

Ecuador has ten mountains over 5,000 m/16,400 ft high, nine of which have glaciers. The Big Ten are all volcanoes and lie in the north of the country where there are two volcanic chains. However, the term *chain* is misleading. Being volcanoes, the mountains stand alone, which makes their access easy. The two chains are separated by high valleys called the Sierra, as described in Alexander von Humboldt's *Valley of the Volcanoes:* "The Sierra averages 2,500 m/8,200 ft high and is made up of a series of ten basins called *hoyas*. To the west of the Sierra are the coastal plains *(la Costa)* and the Pacific Ocean; to the east *(el Oriente)*, the Amazon jungle."

The two chains on either side of the Sierra are called the Cordillera Occidental (west of Quito) and the Cordillera Real, Central, or Oriental (east of Quito). A number of sub-5,000 m/16,400 ft peaks are in the middle, which is called the Interandean region, and a couple are out east in the jungle. The two chains are 40 km/25 mi to 60 km/38 mi apart, so there is little practical sense in dividing the two chains and the bit in the middle, but for the record:

The western Cordillera Occidental runs 360 km/225 mi south-southwest from Chiles on the Colombian border to Chimborazo and includes

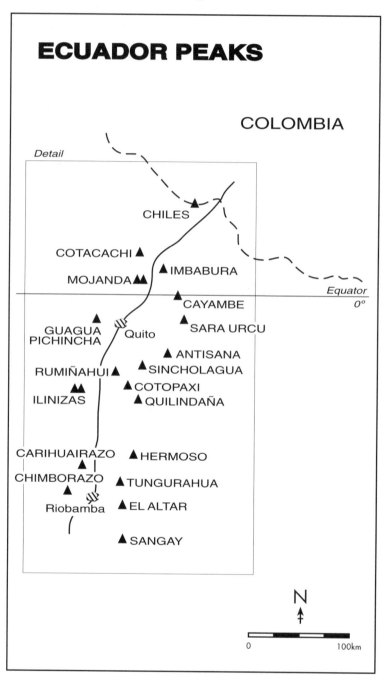

ECUADOR PEAKS

COLOMBIA

Detail

CHILES

COTACACHI

MOJANDA ▲ IMBABURA

Equator
0°

CAYAMBE

GUAGUA
PICHINCHA   Quito   SARA URCU

ANTISANA

RUMIÑAHUI   SINCHOLAGUA

COTOPAXI

ILINIZAS   QUILINDAÑA

CARIHUAIRAZO   HERMOSO

CHIMBORAZO   TUNGURAHUA

Riobamba   EL ALTAR

SANGAY

N

0   100km

Cotacachi, Cuicocha, Pululahua, the Pichinchas above Quito, Atacazo, Corazón, the Ilinizas (originally one volcano), Quilotoa with its crater lake, and Carihuairazo.

The eastern Cordillera Oriental stretches for 350 km/220 mi running roughly parallel to the Cordillera Occidental and includes Cayambe, Antisana, Sincholagua, Cotopaxi, Quilindaña, Tungurahua, El Altar, and Sangay. These volcanoes are relatively young and so more often have the classic volcanic cone shape. The more active volcanoes, such as Cotopaxi, Tungurahua, and Sangay, are nearly perfectly symmetrical.

The Interandean region includes the mountains Rumiñahui, Pasochoa, Mojanda, and Imbabura, all of which are relatively young and potentially active. To the east, in the jungle, are two active volcanoes, Reventador and Sumaco.

A CLIMBING HISTORY

There is no evidence of pre-Hispanic climbing in Ecuador, unlike in Peru and Chile, beyond several hill forts *(pucaras)* located on the top of Pambamarca (4,075 m/13,369 ft) and some ruins on Corazón (4,788 m/ 15,708 ft). The first recorded climbing in Ecuador was on July 29, 1582, when José Toribio de Ortiguera and five other Spaniards climbed Guagua Pichincha (4,794 m/15,728 ft), the active volcano above Quito, to have a look at the crater.

The Spanish did not allow any foreign expeditions into Ecuador until 1736 when a Franco-Spanish scientific expedition arrived to establish the length of a degree of latitude on the equator. French geographer and mathematician Charles Marie de la Condamine led the expedition, accompanied by countrymen Pierre Bouguer and Louis Godin and Spaniards Jorge Juan and Antonio de Ulloa. The expedition stayed in Ecuador until 1744 and marked out a base line 8 km/5 mi long to the northwest of Quito and then began triangulating using a number of high points, including the summit of Pichincha, where they spent 23 days in 1737. They climbed the then snow-capped Corazón (4,788 m/15,708 ft) in 1738, thereby establishing the altitude record for Europeans—Mont Blanc (4,807 m/15,771 ft) was not climbed until 1786. Condamine wanted to climb Cotopaxi, but no one would go with him, so he had to be satisfied with being on the volcano during an eruption. He also reached 4,745 m/ 15,567 ft on Chimborazo and declared it to be the highest mountain in the world—which it is. If you measure the distance from the center of the planet to the summit, Chimborazo is in fact 2,229 m/7,313 ft higher than Mount Everest.

Condamine's expedition raised Ecuador's international profile among geographers, thus encouraging a succession of expeditions, including one led by the German scientific explorer Alexander von Humboldt—the "father of modern geography"—accompanied by Frenchman Aimé Goujaud (called Bonpland) and Ecuadorian Carlos Montúfar. In 1802, Humboldt claimed to reach 5,878 m/19,286 ft on Chimborazo—this was only sixteen years after the first ascent of Mont Blanc. It is now believed that he reached a maximum of 5,640 m/18,500 ft, but this was still the highest point yet reached by a European. Humboldt's account of the climb helped make the mountain one of the most famous in the world. According to Humboldt, it was not until 1820 that a higher mountain was identified.

The Venezuelan liberator of South America, Simón Bolívar, described Chimborazo as "The Watch Tower of the Universe" and spent a night on the mountain in 1822. The experience led him to write his poem *El Delirio*. In 1831 Bolívar's friend French geographer Joseph-Dieudonné Boussingault claimed to have reached 6,004 m/19,698 ft on Chimborazo, a new altitude record for westerners (or northerners, depending on your point of view), accompanied by Colonel Francis Hall (U.S.) and an unnamed climber identified in the literature as "a Negro." It is now thought that Boussingault got about 200 m/660 ft higher than Humboldt. Boussingault also attempted Cotopaxi with Hall.

In 1856 Jules Remy (France) and Mr. Brenchley (U.K.) claimed to have reached the summit in zero visibility. Their calculations, which were based on the boiling point of water, indicated that they had reached 6,543 m/21,466 ft, and Humboldt had measured the mountain at 6,544 m/21,469 ft. Writing in the *Journal of Botany and Kew Gardens Miscellany* (1857), and quoted by Edward Whymper in the *Alpine Journal* (1880–82), Remy states: "When we had calculated our observations, we made the unexpected and gratifying discovery that we had stood on the summit of Chimborazo, without being aware of it." Whymper dismissed the calculations, Remy admitted his thermometer was faulty, and no one else appears to have supported this first claim to reach the summit of Chimborazo.

Cotopaxi became the first of Ecuador's Big Ten peaks to be climbed in 1872—thereby disproving Humboldt's statement that the ascent was impossible. Wilhelm Reiss (Germany) and Angel María Escobar (Colombia) reached the crater rim by following lava flows "like climbing stairs." Baron Max von Thielmann later climbed to the crater and wrote in the *Alpine Journal* (1878), "Its ascent is not much more difficult than Primrose Hill" (a popular Sunday stroll for Londoners). In 1877 there was a massive eruption of Cotopaxi and three months later the German Teodoro Wolf and Ecuadorian Alejandro Sandoval made the first modern ascent, starting from Limpiopungo to the north of the mountain, the direction of the present-day Normal Route. A number of other ascents took place, but none of them are thought to have reached the highest point, a 45-m/150-ft pinnacle of rock or ice, depending on conditions. The first ascent of the pinnacle, which no longer exists, is claimed for the Swede Gunnar Eklund, who climbed from the east in 1929.

Reiss, together with another German, Alphons Stübel, spent two years in Colombia from 1868 to 1870 studying volcanoes before moving south to Ecuador where they spent five years exploring and climbing. In 1869 they made the first ascent of Chiles on the Ecuador-Colombia border, and during 1870 they summited Pichincha, Atacazo, Corazón, and Yana Urco and made attempts on Rumiñahui and Cotacachi. In 1871 they climbed Imbabura and Las Puntas and visited Chimborazo. They calculated its height as 6,310 m/20,702 ft, the height generally accepted today (although precise measurements by a British military expedition in 1993 found the height to be 6,268 m/20,564 ft, similar to Condamine's calculation of 6,276 m/20,590 ft made 250 years earlier). That year, Reiss and Stübel also visited the Ilinizas and Antisana. In February 1873 they made the first ascent of Tungurahua, and 10 days later Stübel made the second ascent of Cotopaxi, less than four months after Reiss made the first ascent. Stübel went on to get close enough to Cerro Hermoso in the Llanganates to measure it.

On December 9, 1879, the British conqueror of the Matterhorn, Edward Whymper, arrived in Guayaquil accompanied by his rival for the Matterhorn, Italian guide Jean-Antoine Carrel, his cousin Louis Carrel, and eleven barometers. During Whymper's victorious descent from the Matterhorn in 1865, four climbers had slipped and fallen to their deaths. The criticism surrounding this tragic event was intense, and Whymper gave up mountaineering as sport. He became interested in studying the effects of high altitude—the concept of mountain sickness was not universally accepted—and this new activity gave him a justifiable excuse to climb. He planned an expedition to the Himalayas in 1874, but the political situation in India led him to cancel the trip. He then considered Peru, where the highest peaks outside the Himalayas had been found, but Peru and Bolivia went to war against Chile in 1879 in the War of the Pacific thereby ending plans for that trip. Whymper wrote: "I turned to the Republic of Ecuador, the most lofty remaining country which was accessible" (*Travels Amongst the Great Andes of the Equator,* 1892).

In 1880, Whymper and the Carrels started with the first ascent of Chimborazo in a continuous 16-hour push, up and down, that left Louis Carrel with frostbitten feet—it was seven weeks before he could climb again. The climb made the trio the first Europeans to summit a major peak higher than 6,100 m/20,000 ft. (Frenchman Charles Wiener climbed a 6,131-m/20,115-ft subsidiary peak of Illimani in Bolivia in 1877.) There were six other first ascents—Sincholagua, Antisana, Cayambe, Sara Urcu (not climbed again until 1955), Cotacachi, and Carihuairazo—before they returned to make the second ascent of Chimborazo by a different route accompanied by Ecuadorians David Beltrán and Francisco Javier Campaña. The group saw an eruption of Cotopaxi that left Chimborazo's summit covered in ash and turned day to night. The second ascent was faster than the first and so added to the theory that acclimatization is beneficial. The Carrels claimed to reach the top of Iliniza Sur, but Whymper failed on two attempts. The three also spent a night just below Cotopaxi's crater rim prior to a successful ascent. Mountaineering historian Walt Unsworth in *Hold the Heights* (1993) states: "He had demonstrated that by careful planning and management it was possible for a mountaineering expedition to be mounted to distant and difficult parts of the globe with complete success." Whymper's book of the trip, *Travels Amongst the Great Andes of the Equator* (1892), remains one of the all-time mountaineering classics.

The "father" of Ecuadorian climbing, Nicolás Martínez (1874–1934), made the third ascent of Antisana in 1904 accompanied to the glacier by Lorenzo Guaigua, a guide whom Martínez says was 120 years old at the time and was still alive 15 years later. Martínez made the fifth ascent of Tungurahua in 1905 at a time when a snow camp was needed, and also that year he made the seventh ascent of Cotopaxi, getting lost and then snow-blind on the descent. At this time Cotopaxi normally had a smoke plume rising from its crater and climbers risked asphyxiation from sulfurous gases. In 1911 he made the fourth ascent of Chimborazo.

Martínez's most significant climb was the first ascent of Iliniza Norte in 1912, in which he survived earthquake-induced rockfall, after failing to climb on the same trip Quilindaña (not climbed until 1952) and Iliniza Sur (not repeated after the Carrels' 1880 ascent until 1939 when Germans Gottfried Hirtz, Dmitri Kakabadse, and Wilfrid Kühm summited). Martínez's ascent made Iliniza Norte the only one of the Big Ten to be climbed first by Ecuadorians, but he deserves his title for doing more than anyone else to popularize climbing in Ecuador through his books and newspaper articles.

The ascent of Iliniza Norte left two of Ecuador's Big Ten peaks unclimbed—Sangay and El Altar.

Sangay is the most continuously active volcano in the world. Whymper saw it erupting from afar and described it as "an active volcano which seems to be known only by name" (*Travels,* 1892), adding that he was not aware that anyone had reached the base of the mountain and he had never gotten a good enough view to fix the mountain's position. Unknown to Whymper, in December 1849 Frenchman Sebastian Wisse had explored the approaches to Sangay and gotten close enough to count 267 eruptions in one hour. The mountain was quiet from 1916 to 1934, allowing the first serious attempts to climb it.

In 1924 the British explorer "Commander" George Dyott climbed Tungurahua (where he witnessed an explosion) and went on to climb the jungle volcano Sumaco. He attempted Sangay in 1925 with another British adventurer, Gilbert Johnston, and reached the glacier but failed to summit in two attempts, getting snow-blind on the first and stuck in an ice field on the second while Johnston was stricken with altitude sickness.

The first group to reach the crater summit was a zoological expedition from the United States, which spent three hours on the rim. Writing in the *American Alpine Journal* (1929–32), Robert Moore explained why Sangay had remained unclimbed: "It is not the altitude which has prevented the attempts on its summit during the past two centuries from proving successful. The cause lies in three things: first, the labyrinth of mighty ash canyons which circle it on the three approachable sides with 500 square miles of difficult terrain; second, meteorological conditions which maintain almost constantly a pall of mist and cloud over the whole area and render even the locating of the volcano difficult; and third, the superstitious fears of the native Indians who never explore the labyrinth of canyons and on whom one must depend for cargo bearers."

Moore and companions spent 28 days getting in to and then climbing the mountain, including 18 days of continuous rain—they managed to keep up the attempt only by eating deer and the now-endangered tapir. Moore's team went on to climb Chimborazo, spending a night on the Veintemilla Summit at 6,267 m/20,561 ft—the highest anyone had camped anywhere in the world to that date.

British mountaineer Chris Bonington climbed Sangay twice in 1966. The first time he used a machete for 9 days to cut a way through from Macas in the east. He comments in his book *The Next Horizon* (1973): "We could have been on a set for Conan Doyle's *Lost World* and it continued to rain as though it would never stop. . . . It was like going up a giant slag-heap, and in the swirling mist it could have been somewhere in the smog of a South Wales coal field. . . . The heads of our ice-axes were stained a dull yellow-green, and I couldn't help wondering what effect the fumes had had on our lungs."

Bonington, partner Sebastian Snow, and Ecuadorian guide Jorge Larrea summited, but they ran out of food, and they had not gotten any photographs for the magazine for which Bonington was working, so they had to go in again. This time they followed the Normal Route—although they were delayed in Alao for 3 days waiting for a fiesta to finish. The most disastrous Sangay expedition was in August 1976 when six Britons attempted the mountain. Two were killed, and three were seriously injured.

In the meantime, a German expedition found and climbed Cerro Hermoso in the Llanganates in 1941 and Quilindaña was climbed in 1952 by a multinational group made up of Italians, a Colombian, a German, a Frenchman, and Arturo Eichler, a German who had settled in Ecuador.

Eichler was forced to flee Germany in 1935 and by chance ended up in Ecuador where he formed an anti-Nazi group. Eichler climbed Rucu Pichincha a number of times, Chimborazo, Sincholagua, and Rumiñahui, and he made the first ascent of the highest peak on Carihuairazo as well as exploring the jungle. His classic book *Nieve y Selva en Ecuador* (1952) included the first climbing chronology of Ecuador and declared Cotopaxi to be 6,005 m/19,701 ft.

It was not until 1963 that the last of Ecuador's Big Ten mountains was climbed—El Altar, a volcano with the west side blown out leaving a horseshoe shape and nine separate peaks higher than 5,000 m/16,400 ft.

Humboldt, Reiss, and Stübel; Whymper and the Carrels; and Hans Meyer (the first person to summit Kilimanjaro in 1889) all explored the mountain without reaching any of the major summits, although Reiss and

Stübel reached a forepeak on Canónigo. It was Meyer who used the religious names for the mountain's separate peaks: Obispo (Bishop), Monja (Nun), Fraile (Friar), Tabernáculo (Tabernacle), and Canónigo (Canon). The first ascent claimed was in 1939 by the German Wilfrid Kühm and the Italians Piero Ghiglione and Isidoro Formaggio, but it is impossible to say what they climbed. The *American Alpine Journal* (1972–73) states that they in fact climbed the Cubillín peaks, which lie 10 km/6 mi to the south.

In 1961 a Japanese expedition from Waseda University reached subsidiary peaks on both Obispo and Canónigo, and in 1962 a number of Ecuadorian climbers failed on Obispo. The next year an Italian expedition arrived under Marino Tremonti and succeeded on Obispo, the highest of the peaks, returning in 1965 to make the first ascent of Canónigo, the second-highest peak in the group. In 1971 a German expedition climbed Monja Chica and 3 days later Tabernáculo. The next year Tremonti was back again with his guides to make the first ascent of Fraile Grande. Ecuadorians Bernardo Beate, Jacinto Carrasco, and Rafael Terán climbed Fraile Beato in 1974, and four years later Beate and Terán made the first ascent of Fraile Oriental. The last of El Altar's peaks to be climbed was Fraile Central in 1979 by a group of six Ecuadorians: Fernando Jaramillo, Luis Naranjo, Danny Moreno, Milton Moreno, Hernán Reinoso, and Mauricio Reinoso.

El Altar remains a test bed for climbers, and it has many hard new-route possibilities. Only two of its nine peaks have been climbed from inside the caldera: in January 1984 the north face of Obispo was climbed (the hardest route yet done in Ecuador) and in December 1984 the south face of Canónigo. Neither route has been repeated.

Another feat awaiting repeat is the climbing of El Altar's nine peaks in one continuous push. Between September 15 and October 5, 1995, Ecuadorians Oswaldo Alcócer, Oswaldo Freire, Gabriel Llano, and Edison Oña were the first to do the so-called "integral," which involved climbing a peak and then descending, moving camp, and repeating. Eight camps were needed, and seven days were lost because of bad weather.

Ecuadorian Climbers

Nicolás Martínez was not happy with the contemporary state of Ecuadorian mountaineering and reportedly said: "Our native laziness and our characteristic apathy have made us contemplate with absolute indifference the immaculate peaks that dare to rise up and conquer the heights"

(*Exploraciones en los Andes Equatorianos,* 1932). However, and largely because of his influence, Ecuadorian climbing became and has remained very healthy, especially compared to the other Andean countries. Just how strong was shown by the rapid repeat of the first ascent of Obispo in December 1963, less than six months after the first ascent and the first ascents of the remaining difficult El Altar peaks during the 1970s.

During the 1940s, the first Ecuadorian climbing clubs were established. Grupo Ascencionismo de San Gabriel has continued producing some of the country's best climbers since its inception, including Ramiro Naverette, who died descending his second Himalayan 8,000-m/26,000-ft peak in 1987.

The relatively popular nature of the sport and recognition of the economic importance of tourism led to the construction of the first mountain hut in 1964 on Chimborazo. Further construction of huts on several of the mountains, along with easy access from Quito and the other Sierra cities, means that the mountains are in reach of a greater number of people than in, say, Peru or Bolivia. Every year Ecuadorian climbers travel to Peru, Bolivia, and Argentina to climb hard routes; guide Ivan Vallejo climbed Manaslu in the Himalayas in 1997, and in 1998 he climbed another 8,000-m/26,000-ft mountain, Broad Peak. In 1999 he summited Mount Everest.

While new routes are explored and climbed by Ecuadorian climbers, there are still other possibilities waiting for those who want to put up new routes.

HIGHLAND GEOLOGY

The volcanoes of Ecuador have given the country universal fame among the geologists of the world. They are the terror of the Indians, the admiration of the conquistadores, the study of naturalists and the plague of the people who live near them.

Teodoro Wolf
Geografía y Geología del Ecuador (1892)

Geology in Ecuador is about volcanoes. The country is full of them—fifty-five to be precise. All ten of the mountains over 5,000 m/16,400 ft are volcanoes, and even the Galápagos Islands are volcanic. Ecuador's volcanoes and the whole of the Andes are a result of the collision between the Pacific Nazca tectonic plate, which is moving eastward at a rate

Burning near Cayambe

of 6 cm/2 in a year, and the South American plate, which is moving west at 3 cm/1 in a year. All the important volcanoes are in the northern part of the country. The south is also of volcanic origin, but at present there is no volcanic activity south of Sangay.

Ecuador's northern volcanoes started life three to four million years ago and are termed *stratovolcanoes*—the cones are made by an accumulation of rock, ash, and lava ejected from the volcano. Thousands of years of continual activity are needed to form the classic volcanic cone with slopes of 30° to 35° with a crater on top. Chimborazo, Rumiñahui, and Rucu Pichincha are also stratovolcanoes, but they have been subject to more erosion and so have lost their conical shape.

Continuing research has changed the definition of what constitutes an active volcano. During the 1970s it was thought that only eight of Ecuador's volcanoes were active. Now twenty-six are classified as active—the latest being Cayambe, which was declared active in 1997 after historians found a description of ash coming out of the volcano and falling on the surrounding area in 1585. It is now held that if a volcano has been active in the last ten thousand years, then there is some probability that it will erupt again.

Eleven volcanoes are permanently monitored for seismic activity, including Cotopaxi, Tungurahua, Guagua Pichincha, Chimborazo, Antisana, and Cayambe. Risk maps are drawn up showing the areas that vulcanologists believe will be affected by eruptions.

A number of volcanoes have erupted in historic times, that is, since the Spanish arrived in 1532. There are written records of eruptions for Cotopaxi (thirty-five since 1534), Tungurahua (twenty-six), Reventador (twenty-five), Guagua Pichincha (three), Quilotoa (one), Antisana (two), and now Cayambe (one). On top of this, Sangay is deemed to be the most continuously active volcano in the world, recording up to four hundred eruptions in one day.

In the last three thousand years it is thought that two other volcanoes have been active: Pululahua (just north of the Mitad del Mundo center) and Cuicocha (now at the base of Cotacachi). The rest of the volcanoes are thought to have been dormant for tens of thousands of years—although this does not mean they won't blow again. Three Ecuadorian volcanoes began erupting in 1999; the renewed activity of Guagua Pichincha and Tungurahua has resulted in the evacuation of towns and villages.

The Ecuadorian Sierra is the result of volcanic phenomena that come in a variety of forms and can change the whole landscape, often in the course of a single eruption.

Pyroclastic flows. These flows are made up of incandescent gas clouds full of pumice stone and ash with temperatures up to 1,000°C/1,800°F. They can move downhill very quickly—during the 1980 Mount St. Helens eruption in the United States, a pyroclastic flow clocked an average speed of 230 kmh/144 mph. A flow can merely carry ash, but it can also pick up rock, mud, and anything else lying in its path. Huge areas have been covered to a depth of hundreds of meters/yards by such flows. Quilindaña is at the center of a huge caldera, called Chalupas, 18 km/11 mi across and up to 400 m/1,300 ft deep. A pyroclastic flow 230,000 years ago covered an area of 2,000 km²/800 sq mi to 3,000 km²/1,200 sq mi. If this happened today it would completely change the Sierra, erasing the current topography and life. It appears that an eruption of Quilotoa did wipe out a civilization—not an impossible event. In 1902, a pyroclastic flow from an eruption of Mount Pelée in Martinique killed thirty thousand people in twelve minutes. Such destructive power leaves areas relatively flat because the flow fills in the valleys (although wind and water subsequently erode these areas). Paradoxically, the flatness of the land encourages new population settlement—it is estimated that forty thousand people now live on the remains of pyroclastic flows from the Cuicocha volcano.

Cone collapse. The causes of volcanic cone collapses are not fully understood, but they can include a cone getting too high or too steep, water seeping in, and earthquakes. The effects are quite impressive, with huge amounts of material being thrown out in a rock avalanche. An amphitheater, or caldera is left, centered on the site of the old cone— as happened to Mount St. Helens in 1980. El Altar, Tungurahua, Chimborazo, Imbabura, Cotopaxi, Reventador, and Pichincha have all suffered collapses, but not in historic times. Some fifty thousand years ago a collapse of Chimborazo created an avalanche that extended 35 km/22 mi and covered an area of 250 km²/100 sq mi. The avalanche created a lake that at one time measured 10 km²/4 sq mi and lasted for centuries. About three thousand years ago, the east side of Tungurahua collapsed at possibly 100 m/330 ft per second, affecting an area of 98 km²/40 sq mi, emitting 8 km³ of loose material—nearly three times as much as the 1980 Mount St. Helens collapse. Collapses do not happen very often in the life of a volcano.

Lahars. Another formative (and destructive) volcanic occurrence is the creation of lahars. These are formed when an eruption melts the snow and ice on a glaciated volcano or the debris hits a lake or river. The resulting mixture of pyroclastic material, ash, mud, and lava is carried by the water, enabling the lahar to travel quickly and a long way—the 1980 Mount St. Helens eruption produced a lahar that moved at 70 kmh/ 44 mph. An eruption of Cotopaxi on June 26, 1877, melted a huge amount of snow and ice, creating a lahar that in 18 hours had traveled 300 km/190 mi and reached Esmeraldas on the Pacific Coast. Edward Whymper reported an account of the eruption:

"Some inhabitants of Mulalo, however, were looking at the summit at 10 A.M., and all at once saw molten lava pouring through the gaps and notches in the lip of the crater, bubbling and smoking, so they described it, like the froth of a pot that suddenly boils over. The scene which then ensued upon the mountain was shut out from mortal eyes, for in a few minutes the whole of it was enveloped in smoke and steam, and became invisible; but out of the darkness a moaning noise arose, which grew into a roar, and a deluge of water, blocks of ice, mud and rock rushed down, sweeping away everything that lay in its course, and leaving a desert in its rear" (*Travels*, 1892).

Lava flows. These flows change the topography, but at a slower rate than other volcanic events. Normally, they follow existing valleys, but they can create a ridge or sometimes even a peak, such as Sincholagua. Important lava flows that have occurred since the Spanish arrived include flows from Cotopaxi, Sangay, Reventador, Antisana, and Tungurahua. The road from Riobamba to Baños passes through the remains of many flows as does the access to Antisana, where the flow is being broken up and carried off to be used for construction material.

Domes. Another feature of a volcanic eruption is a dome that normally forms from the viscous magma in the center of a caldera, showing that a volcano can still be active following a big eruption. Guagua Pichincha has a number of domes, with one building and expected to blow again. Also, the islands in the Cuicocha Lake are domes.

Ash flows. Eruptions are invariably accompanied by large eruptive clouds that can ascend tens of kilometers/miles into the sky and carry tons of ash and pumice. Subsequently, this rock material falls out of the clouds and returns to earth. Large areas are covered in fine ash, including crops and pastureland, which makes it useless for years afterwards. An eruption of Guagua Pichincha in 1660 left Quito in darkness for 4 days and buried under a layer of ash 40 cm/15 in thick. The weight of the ash can collapse roofs and buildings. From 1998 into 2000, Quito was on Yellow Alert, the second of a four-level scale, owing to the increased activity of Guagua Pichincha, which included ejections of ash and vapor and earth tremors. Embassies warned foreign residents to be prepared and store emergency supplies, such as water, flashlights, radios, gas masks, and goggles. The French embassy had prepaid reservations for the use of an entire hacienda near Cayambe in the event that the volcano blew. The mountain began erupting in October 1999, and as expected, it blew out to the west in the opposite direction from Quito. The city did not escape the ashfall, however, as high winds carried the pulverized volcanic ashes back over the city. The ash is very destructive to machinery such as airplane engines, so Quito airport closes for hours or even days following periods of ashfall. Motorized street sweepers cannot clean up ashfall because their air filters clog, so on one notable occasion, four thousand people were given brooms and they swept the runway clean in 4 days.

There are some advantages to all this volcanic activity: the soil is rich, and there's lots of rock for construction work. However, volcanic soil is subject to rapid erosion, which is a big and growing problem in Ecuador. Population pressure is leading to the expansion of cultivation into higher and higher elevations, where the volcanic soil is less capable of sustaining agriculture.

GLACIERS

Cotopaxi shews no signs of approaching decrepitude, and for many centuries yet to come it may remain the highest active volcano in the world; or perchance the imprisoned forces may find an easier outlet, through barriers offering less resistance, and either Sangai, Tungurahua, or Pichincha may become the premier volcano of the Equator. Whilst the great cone which has so often trembled with subterranean thunders—buried beneath glaciers more extensive than those of Cayambe or Antisana—will echo with the crash of the ice-avalanche; its crater will disappear, and, over its rugged floor and its extinguished fires, soft snowflakes will rear a majestic dome loftier than Chimborazo.

Edward Whymper
Travels Amongst the Great Andes of the Equator (1892)

In four years, one of Antisana's glaciers has lost 10 percent of its length—200 m/660 ft—and is now receding at an average of 30 m/100 ft per year. Two Ecuadorian glaciers, one on Antisana and the other on Carihuairazo, are being carefully studied by the French scientific organization Orstom to find out what is happening and at what rate of speed. This is not just a theoretical study: the glaciers provide water for the millions of people who live in Quito and the central Sierra, especially during the dry seasons when there is not enough rainfall to provide a sufficient water supply.

Glaciers in temperate areas like the Rockies and the Alps benefit from winter conditions during the months of October through June when temperatures are low and precipitation on the glaciers is in the form of snow. This leads to the growth of glaciers—a process called accumulation. During the relatively short glacial summer from July through September, temperatures are high, sunlight is more direct, and precipitation is lower and in the form of rain. This leads to a net loss in the size of the glaciers through melting and evaporation—a process called ablation.

Tropical glaciers, like those in Ecuador, do not benefit from a winter period of accumulation. The sun is much more powerful all year, and air temperatures vary little throughout the year. Seasons are relative; the differences between dry and wet seasons are not great. As a result, ablation continues year round. This means tropical glaciers do not get an annual chance to recover and are therefore more sensitive to changes in temperature.

Measurements of the temperature of the Pacific Ocean, the dominant factor in regional weather patterns, show that temperatures are rising. The hot/cold cycle referred to as El Niño/La Niña has become skewed. Instead of alternating hot/cold years, we are now experiencing successive hot years—five successive hot years in the late 1990s and then the start of a cold period in 1998. The reason for this change in the cycle is the global warming caused by air pollution—the twentieth century was the warmest in the last twelve thousand years. No one knows when or if this trend will reverse, but glacial measurements from across the world show an accelerated rate of glacial retreat since the early 1980s, which then increased yet further in the 1990s.

The higher temperatures increase precipitation on the coast, and as a result coastal Ecuador gets whipped by destructive storms. But the Sierra suffers from lower than normal rates of precipitation. This together with the higher temperatures leads to an increase in the rate of evaporation and melting that causes the glaciers to recede faster. However, figures also show that during the wetter periods a high rate of melting occurs, and

Chimborazo from Obispo, El Altar

glaciers in the wetter areas are in fact receding faster than others.

Glaciers are made up of two parts: the accumulation zone (where the glacier forms) and the ablation zone (where the glacier disappears). Glaciologists calculate a line for the point where accumulation and ablation zones meet—the Equilibrium Line Altitude (ELA). The writings about and pictures of Condamine, Humboldt, Whymper, and others are being closely examined to provide information about the ELA during the eighteenth and nineteenth centuries, while photographs can provide valuable information about the twentieth century. Around fourteen thousand to twelve thousand years ago, everything above 4,400 m/14,400 ft was covered by glaciers. When Condamine was in Ecuador in 1738, the ELA was about 4,750 m/15,580 ft. It is now calculated at 5,050 m/16,570 ft and rising. This means that any glaciers below this level are receding, and those whose tops are below this height are in a process of terminal recession. Orstom studies of the Chacaltaya glacier at 5,390 m/17,680 ft in Bolivia have led to the prediction that the glacier will completely disappear by 2014. If present trends are maintained, and there is nothing to suggest they won't be, the glaciers on Sara Urcu, Tungurahua, and Carihuairazo will be gone within twenty years, those on Iliniza Sur will have virtually disappeared, and those on El Altar will have shrunken considerably.

HIGHLAND NATURAL HISTORY

When the two Andean mountain chains (*cordilleras*) rose up in what is now Ecuador, the existing plants and animals were isolated into three separate regions: the coast, the Sierra, and the Amazon. The coastal and Amazonian sides of the western and eastern cordilleras have very similar microclimates—they are both very humid—while the western and eastern highlands above the central valley (Sierra), protected on both sides by mountains, are much drier. The Ecuadorian highlands have twin systems of flora and fauna in the Andean woodlands (*bosques andinos*) and high grasslands (*páramo*) that go from the woodlands to the snow line. As a result, plants and animals from different families performing the same functions have adapted to similar conditions in the different areas.

Mammals

There aren't many camelids left in Ecuador. Llamas are being reintroduced in the Cotopaxi National Park, and a vicuña project is underway between Chimborazo and Carihuairazo where these animals are being reintroduced from Chilean herds. Llamas are not very pleasant creatures, as Edward Whymper noted: "One day, Jean-Antoine and I came upon a tame llama, browsing by the side of a lane. It was the first my companion had seen, and he approached the animal to stroke its nose; but alas, when he was within a couple of yards, the gentle creature reared its pretty head and spat in his face" (*Travels*, 1892).

Llamas fight, belch, chase dogs, and are generally worth avoiding. *Vicuñas* are smaller than llamas and have much shorter hair—they look like antelope—and are very timid.

Andean foxes (*lobo de páramo*—literally, high grasslands wolf) will come up to camps scavenging for food, and they will happily steal any left around—especially in the Cotopaxi National Park and around Antisana. They tend to have larger, bushier tales than their Northern Hemisphere counterparts.

More mammals live in the lower highland areas with its more plentiful vegetation that provides food and cover. Wetter and wilder areas lacking human colonization in the eastern parts of the eastern cordillera provide habitat for a number of large but hard-to-see mammals. In these areas it is quite common to see deer droppings from the white-tailed deer (*venado*) and occasionally the beasts themselves, or rather their backsides as they bound rapidly away.

The heaviest native mammal in Ecuador is the woolly mountain tapir, which is in danger of extinction. They are the symbol for the particularly wet Sangay National Park, and you could easily assume them to have scales rather than fur given their habitat. They have a very distinctive, angular footprint. The first successful expedition to Sangay managed to maintain the attempt only by eating deer and tapir. Another explanation for the declining numbers of tapir was suggested in the early 1970s by scientists who investigated the Sangay area and found tapir tracks of various sizes and ages leading up ash slopes on the active volcano but none coming down. A project to monitor numbers by placing radio-collars on tapir backfired when it was discovered that local people found it very easy to obtain equipment to track the animals and kill them.

Just as rare, and sharing similar habitats, is the spectacled bear, which has been seen in the Sangay and Sara Urcu areas, among others. Even rarer is the puma, or mountain lion, which hunts alone and at night, making it very difficult to see, although its pawprints are sometimes seen in the morning after it has passed by.

Birds

The biggest highland bird is the condor. They are quite spectacularly big with wingspans of up to 3 m/10 ft—the largest of any land bird. The huge wings are not flapped while in flight—the great birds circle up using thermals. If one soars past closely, you can hear a strange whirring sound from the tips of the wings. Apart from sheer size, a condor is recognizable by its white neck ruff and the silver-white color of the upper surface of its wings. If you are close to one, you can see its ugly, bald red head—easy for it to clean after a carcass-stripping session. The image of grace and power that condors have when in the air is lost when they land—they hop around in a clumsy, uncoordinated way. They gorge themselves on carrion to the extent that they cannot fly until they have digested the feast. This makes them easy targets for hunters who bait them with carcasses, lie in wait, and then pounce after the birds have eaten. (Hunting condors is illegal.)

Another carrion-eater is the carunculated caracara, the most beautiful of the big birds regularly seen in the highlands. It has a yellow beak, red face, black upperparts and neck, white underparts, and yellow claws. The birds come to camps to hunt for scraps and are often seen along roadsides waiting for roadkill to eat. Numerous raptors are seen also, including the variable hawk and the buzzard eagle, which has long broad wings and a short wedge-shaped tail.

The very noisy Andean gulls (*gaviota*) seem to enjoy the *páramo* even though it is a long way from the sea. Slightly less noisy are Andean lapwings, which have a distinctive white bar across the upper surface of their wings, seen as a V-shape when they take off. The strangest noise is made by the Andean snipe, which is a night flier—it sounds rather disturbingly like the whirring sound made by falling rock.

The name *Quito* comes from the word *Quitolt,* meaning "land of hummingbirds." They are seen surprisingly high up, often to within a few hundred meters of the snow line. The largest hummingbird in the world is the giant hummingbird, which is found up to 3,500 m/11,500 ft. The hummingbird that lives at the highest elevation is the Chimborazo hillstar. To survive the low nighttime temperatures, it drops its body temperature from 39.5°C/103°F to 15°C/59°F and its heartbeat from 1,200 beats per minute to 40 beats per minute. One subspecies of this hummingbird is restricted to Chimborazo, hence its scientific name *Oreotrochilus chimborazo chimborazo.* It has been seen flying close to the refuge at 5,000 m/16,000 ft.

Flora

Originally, the whole of the Sierra was covered by Andean woodland (*bosque andino*), a biodiverse ecosystem. Human settlement began around ten thousand years ago, and as areas of woodland were cleared for cultivation, the higher areas lost their tree cover forever, leaving behind the *páramo* grasslands. The arrival of the Spanish in the sixteenth century drastically accelerated the destruction of the Andean woodlands because the animals they brought over (cows, horses, pigs, sheep, and goats) could not survive on the tough native grasses. The Spanish burned the existing grasses so their animals could eat the fresh green shoots that sprang up afterwards. As a result, original *bosque andino* has virtually disappeared from the Sierra and is found extensively only on the western side of the western cordillera and the eastern side of the eastern cordillera.

Plants have adopted various techniques to survive in the dry, cold, and windy conditions of the *páramo* and above. Often the leaf surface is waxy to reduce transpiration, the leaves are small, and sometimes there are no stems so that they cannot be frozen. The most noticeable exception is the *togro*, which has big fleshy leaves and stems. You would expect this plant to be at risk of freezing; however, the *togro* creates a kind of antifreeze to protect itself. Another survival technique is companionship: a number of different plants grow closely together, using and then putting back different nutrients and minerals into the soil.

The common hard and spiky *páramo* grass is called *ichu*, or *ugsha*. It is used for thatching and floor covering, and llamas also eat it. The green spongy, dry plants are called *almohadas;* they look like pillows (the literal translation) but feel as hard as rock. The leaves never drop, but instead they dry up and provide insulation for the living plant that continues growing on top. Some small mammals and birds nest in them.

The traditional symbol of Ecuadorian climbers is the *chuquirahua*, which has lots of small, spiky dark green leaves and orange flowers that can grow to more than 1 m/3 ft high. A more practical plant for climbers is the *candelaría*, which has a high wax content and burns well even when wet. The *puya*, or *achupaya*, flowers once a year when it sends up a 1.2-m/4-ft- to 2.4-m/8-ft-high stem, which has turquoise flowers. It is a high-altitude member of the pineapple family, and the bottom 5 cm/ 2 in to 8 cm/3 in of the leaves can be eaten. The completely orange-red plants are in fact a moss called *lycopodium*.

Frailejones, high-altitude sunflowers, are seen only in the Páramo El

Angel near Chiles and in the Llanganates. The stems can be 4 m/ 13 ft high, and they often appear to resemble people from a distance— hence the common name Grayfriar. The largest highland tree is the *polylepis*, a member of the rosewood family that grows at altitudes higher than any other species of tree in the world. There are two major sorts of polylepis: in drier areas (above the Sierra) they have paperlike, red- dish bark; in wetter areas (above the coast and the Amazon) the bark is less red and paperlike, and they support mosses and epiphytes.

At lower altitudes, the range of plants is much greater. On the trek up to Tungurahua, you pass through tunnels of bamboo. Up to 4,000 m/ 13,100 ft, you can see *chocho*, a wild lupine with edible seeds. On the way north of Quito, through the Quebrada Guayllabamba, the most striking plant is the *Agava americana*, a large cactus that after ten to fifteen years sprouts one huge stem, often 6 m/20 ft high, which is pollinated by the giant hummingbird. When the stem falls over, it scatters ready-to-grow plantlets, and the parent plant dies. The roots are used for shampoo, soap, and conditioner. The trunk can be cut up and made into drums by stretch- ing leather over the sections. The flower buds are pickled and served as capers. The growing stem can be cut to tap a clear liquid called *chahuamishci*, which is used to cook grains and to drink as it is or after fermenting. The spines can be broken off and used as needles with thread attached. The pounded leaves yield a fiber that can be woven into sacks or twisted into rope.

Agriculturally, the main cultivated crops are potatoes, *oca, melloco, mashua,* sweet corn *(choclo),* fava beans *(habas),* barley *(cebada),* and wheat *(trigo).* A new cash crop is flowers: the Sierra is being taken over by ugly, large plastic greenhouses. Previously, Colombia was the center for this trade, but the drug war has given Ecuador the opportunity to move in on the business and the road to Quito airport is blocked by flower trucks every day during the early hours. Latacunga (population 40,000) now has an international airport just for the export of flowers to the United States and Europe.

The Campamento Mariscal Sucre Museum in the Cotopaxi National Park has a good display of stuffed and preserved examples of highland natural history.

CHAPTER 2

preparations

I was told before departure that everything one could possibly want could be obtained there. It is indeed true that nearly everything may be obtained in Ecuador. It is also true that we often had great difficulty in obtaining anything.

Edward Whymper
Travels Amongst the Great Andes of the Equator (1892)

The capital city of Quito is the logical base for any climbing trip to Ecuador given its altitude of 2,850 m/9,350 ft, its many services, and its ease of access to all the major peaks. (Full access details from Quito are given for all the peaks.) On top of the essentials, the climate is pleasant, the city has a wide range of good places in which to stay and eat, and architecturally the old colonial district *(centro histórico)* is one of the most beautiful parts of any city in South America.

However, Quito is failing to deal with its worsening air pollution and rising crime rate, and this situation is causing visitors to look for alternative places in which to base themselves while in Ecuador. Several regional highland centers have banks, moneychangers, supermarkets, and good places in which to stay and eat. There are also numerous places to stay outside the towns, including some excellent sixteenth- and seventeenth-century haciendas, such as Guachalá near Cayambe and La Ciénega near Lasso.

There are a few supplies or services you can obtain only in Quito. These include maps, white gas, and screw-on Camping Gaz canisters, all major tourism agencies, and consular services. However, starting your trip in Quito gives you the opportunity to take care of all these necessities and then leaves you free to base yourself where you want or to move around and experience more of the country.

Alternative highland bases include the following:

⟶   Otavalo 2,544 m/8,346 ft for Chiles, Cotacachi, Imbabura, Mojanda, Cayambe, and Sara Urcu. (A Supermaxi supermarket is located in Ibarra, 30 minutes by bus from Otavalo.)

⟶   Ambato for Chimborazo and Carihuairazo (from the north), Tungurahua, and Hermoso.

⟶   Riobamba for Chimborazo and Carihuairazo (from the south), El Altar, Tungurahua, and Sangay.

⟶   If you buy supplies beforehand, there are many places to stay between Machachi and Lasso and in the surrounding area for Corazón, Cotopaxi, Rumiñahui, Sincholagua, the Ilinizas, and Quilindaña.

The only mountains for which there are no logical alternative starts other than Quito are Antisana and Guagua Pichincha.

See the general guidebooks (in Appendix C) for detailed information on what each town has to offer.

GETTING THERE

You have a choice of airlines and routes from North America and Europe to Quito, although some are more direct than others. Weight allowances vary between airlines and tend to be much higher with North American carriers; stopover requirements also vary. A more expensive ticket might end up costing less than a cheaper ticket plus excess baggage and stopover costs.

A truck stuck in the mud (for 17 hours) in Cotopaxi National Park

Check with several airlines before purchasing your ticket.

An alternative way to get to Quito is to fly to Guayaquil on the coast (most international flights land at Guayaquil before or after Quito) and then take the train to Riobamba in the Sierra, which gives great views—you ride the roof. Check to make sure the train is running before you plan this trip.

The international exit tax from Ecuador airports is US$25, payable in U.S. dollars or the equivalent in Ecuadorian sucres.

CURRENCY

In March 2000 the Ecuadorian government began using U.S. dollars as well as Ecuadorian sucres as legal tender. The conversion to the use of U.S. dollars as the country's primary currency was expected to take six months or longer. At the time of this writing, both U.S. dollars and Ecuadorian sucres were in use.

VISAS AND PASSPORTS

According to the 1997 *Ley de Turismo*, on entry to Ecuador all tourists are entitled to a 90-day visa (as long as you have not been in the country within the last 12 months). You will also be given a piece of paper with a copy of your entry stamp on it. Do not lose this, or your departure will be delayed.

At Immigrations at the airport in Quito, you will be asked how long you plan to stay. Based on your answer, you will be given a 30-, 60-, or 90-day tourist visa. If necessary, you can later extend a short-term visa up to the maximum amount of 90 days from entry. To do this, on the last working day that your visa is valid, go to the departmental migration office in Quito at the Policía Nacional de Migración de Pichincha located on Isla Seymour and Río Coca.

Passports must have at least six months' validity left. Carry a copy of your passport at all times. You will need the original to get into the Instituto Geográfico Militar to buy maps.

ACCLIMATIZATION

It seemed certain that sooner or later we should suffer like the rest of the world, but I proposed to put off the evil day as long as possible; to mount gradually and leisurely, by small stages, so that there should be no abrupt transition.

Edward Whymper
Travels Amongst the Great Andes of the Equator (1892)

Edward Whymper had the right idea, but he and his guides were all struck down by altitude sickness on Chimborazo: "We were feverish, had intense headaches, and were unable to satisfy our desire for air, except by breathing with open mouths. This naturally parched the throat, and produced a craving for drink, which we were unable to satisfy—partly from the difficulty in obtaining it, and partly from trouble in swallowing it" (*Travels*, 1892).

Fitness is no substitute for acclimatization; indeed, fit young men appear to have more problems than other people. Arrival at the height of Quito (the airport is at 2,812 m/9,226 ft) directly from sea level is a shock for the body. Common symptoms of what is mild altitude sickness include breathlessness, a racing pulse, lethargy, tiredness, an inability to sleep, loss of appetite, headache, and dehydration. These symptoms will normally last for a couple of days.

Some people recommend taking acetazolamide (Diamox) prophylactically, preferably via sustainable-release tablets, starting when you get on the plane at home. Acetazolamide speeds up acclimatization by acidifying the blood, which increases respiration. It improves oxygen transport and helps improve sleep. It acts as a diuretic, so you should drink more clear liquids (excluding alcohol) while taking acetazolamide. It sometimes causes a tingling sensation in the fingers and toes, and people who have a sulfur allergy should not take it. Consult your physician before using acetazolamide, and if you plan to use it for the first time, try some well before your trip to make sure you do not experience unpleasant side effects.

The higher and drier air and the lower pressure available to force the oxygen into your blood in Quito and at all points above mean that you breathe faster than at sea level. As a result, you lose a lot more moisture through respiration. Therefore, you must consciously drink much more than at sea level—bottled mineral and purified water is widely available in Quito. Above 5,000 m/16,000 ft you need more than 5 liters/qts a day. Check the color of your urine, it should be "gin clear" and not Tequila Sunrise orange—the more yellow the urine, the more dehydrated you are.

Your digestive system also needs time to adapt because digestive efficiency falls at high altitude, making fat and protein difficult to digest. Therefore, eat light meals high in carbohydrates and low in fat.

No one knows for sure what causes altitude sickness, but the key to avoiding it seems to be to take it really easy when you arrive. People who rush their acclimatization invariably regret it later. Climbers should spend 5 days at the height of Quito or the equivalent (basically, in the Sierra) before attempting to climb any of the Big Ten. This time can be spent trekking or doing some of the lower climbs. Most but not all climbers will then be ready to go.

It is still possible to get altitude sickness if you ascend to heights at a rate too fast for your body to adjust. This circumstance cannot be foreseen—individuals react to going high in different ways and at different rates. There is a particular danger in Ecuador because of the ease of access to the mountains: in 3 hours you can drive from Quito at 2,850 m/9,350 ft to the Cotopaxi car park at 4,600 m/15,100 ft; in less than 5 hours you can get to the Carrel hut at 4,800 m/15,750 ft on Chimborazo.

The standard acclimatization guidance of 300-m/1,000-ft height gain per day above 3,000 m/10,000 ft with a rest day every fourth day is not followed in Ecuador. If it were, it would take 7 days to get to the Cotopaxi hut from Quito, followed by a rest day and then another 3 days to reach the summit. Cotopaxi is normally done in a round trip from Quito of less than 36 hours.

This means climbers do not acclimatize, but instead climb following the adage "Climb high; sleep low," getting up and down the route as fast as possible before altitude sickness hits. Some people are not physiologically capable of this style of climbing and will suffer altitude sickness that might prevent them from climbing or even kill them.

Spending an extra night at the hut on Cotopaxi, Chimborazo, or Cayambe is not recommended. To acclimatize to these heights takes weeks. All an extra night does is increase the deterioration that your body suffers at high altitude because you are spending more time up high. You will find it difficult to sleep well, and your digestive system will be less efficient. Your mental health, an equally important factor in summit success, will also deteriorate through boredom.

SPANISH

Although it is possible to climb in Ecuador without knowing a word of Spanish—if you pay someone to organize everything for you—your experience will be richer if you can communicate directly. It is a good idea to learn how to count, tell time, and know the days of the week before coming to Ecuador to help with shopping and transport arrangements.

Most tourist agencies, hotel staff, and guides speak English. In the countryside and outside the major tourist destinations, however, people do not understand English or any languages other than Spanish and Quichua.

FOOD

At high altitude the body does not process fat and protein as efficiently as at lower altitudes and neither does it need as much fat and protein as normal. What your body does need is carbohydrates. Food choice is obviously personal, but the most important factor is to have food that you want to eat. Most people experience an extremely reduced desire to eat at high altitude, which works against meeting the huge increase in calorific need.

Try to eat as quickly as possible after returning to the hut or camp. If you eat carbohydrates within 1 hour of finishing exercise, your muscles will recover in the shortest possible time. If you don't eat within 3 hours of finishing exercise, your muscles will deteriorate.

All food necessary for a mountaineering expedition can be bought easily in Quito and the major cities. Cereals, powdered milk, bread, cheese, peanut butter (in plastic jars), jam, good chocolate, powdered drinks, packet soups, chinese noodles, ready-to-eat rice and pasta meals, among other items, are all available. The best chain of supermarkets is Supermaxi; the nearest branches to the center of Quito are in Multicentro on Avenida 6 de Diciembre and La Niña or in El Jardin Mall (open every day until 8 P.M.). (*Note:* The prices in large print are for those with Supermaxi discount cards. The price you pay is the higher one in smaller print.)

Outside Quito, if there isn't a Supermaxi, the range of food available is much smaller, and ready-to-eat rice and pasta meals are difficult or impossible to find. In villages, only the basics are available: pasta, tinned sardines, crackers.

FUEL

Gasoline is cheap (about US$1 per gal/3.5 liters) and widely available. Camping Gaz–style cannisters are available at camping supply shops in Quito and Riobamba. Screw-on Gaz canisters are often available at Hobby at Multicentro, Avenida 6 de Diciembre and La Niña. White gas is very difficult to find. The best place to look for duct tape (*cinta de embalaje*) is Kywi on 10 de Agosto and Cordero.

EQUIPMENT

To paraphrase Edward Whymper, everything you might need is at some-time available from one of the Quito climbing and outdoor shops, but sometimes none of them will have what you want. Duracell MN1203 headlamp batteries, when available, cost about US$8 to $10. Equipment from the United States tends to be cheaper in Ecuador than in Europe, but European gear tends to be very expensive.

Good Quito equipment shops include the following:

➡ Los Alpes, Reina Victoria 821 and Baquedano (tel 232362), open Monday–Friday

➡ Altamontaña, Jorge Washington 425 and 6 de Diciembre (tel 558380), open Monday–Friday

➡ Andean Sport, Roca 549 and Juan Leon Mera (tel 540442), open Monday–Saturday

➡ Andisimo, 9 de Octubre 479 and Roca (tel 223030), open Monday–Friday

➡ Camping Sports, Colón 942 and Reina Victoria (tel 521626), open Monday–Friday

➡ Equipos Cotopaxi, 6 de Diciembre 927 and Patria (tel 500038), open Monday–Friday

➡ The Explorer, Reina Victoria 928 and Pinto (tel 550911), open Monday–Friday

➡ Rivet replacement and restitching of plastic and leather boots can be done at Zapytal, Joaquín Pinto 538 and Amazonas, Quito.

Outside Quito there is a very limited range of equipment; some is available in Riobamba and in Baños, but don't rely on it. See the appendixes for equipment lists, including Spanish translations. For equipment rental, see "Agencies" below.

PHOTOGRAPHY

North American- and European-quality film and processing are available in Quito and major tourist destinations in Ecuador. All types of film and developing are available. If you use slide film, you can get it developed without mounts (solo revelado) for US$2—all developers appear to scratch slide film when mounting it. Slide film costs US$6 to $7, but look around, prices vary a lot between shops. Recommended film processors are Fotorama at Roca and Tamayo in Quito and the Ecuacolor chain. For camera repairs, start at Fotorama, or call Adolfo Alvarez (Quito 236034), who speaks perfect English.

Camera batteries can go flat very quickly at altitude—make sure you've got some spares. Full-on electronic cameras have a tendency to freeze up. Lithium batteries can be difficult to find and expensive—bring a spare.

WHEN TO CLIMB

Some say there are seasons but this is hard to prove.

Michael Koerner
The Fool's Climbing Guide to Ecuador and Peru (1976)

There are two climbing seasons in Ecuador: June through August and December through February. Allegedly, the eastern cordillera is drier December through February and the western cordillera, June through August (though it is often windy in August). Cotopaxi has more clear days than any other peak. It is best to avoid the wetter seasons of March through May and September through November. However, the weather can be good or bad on any day of the year, and it is worth remembering that Whymper's grand tour was December to July. Bad weather is predominant for the mountains on the eastern side of the eastern cordillera (for example, El Altar, Sangay, Llanganates, and Sara Urcu). Because Ecuador is located on the equator, days and nights are 12 hours long. As a result, climbs are attempted all year round all over the country.

More important than the time of year is the time of day you climb—you should aim to reach the summit of any of the snowcapped peaks before 8 A.M. so that descent is completed well before midday. As the snow is warmed by the sun, it attains the consistency of sugar, which makes it hard going and also dangerous—avalanches are far more likely. On top of this, any rock held in place by ice will start its gravity-induced downward journey once the sun has melted the cementing ice. In good weather the heat is so incredible that you want to strip off, but if you do so, you will get the worst sunburn of your life.

Nights and early mornings are generally clear. However, clouds normally come in by midday if not earlier, often reducing visibility to zero. This is another reason to climb at night. If the route is not tracked out by previous parties, it is worth marking the way with flags to help find your way down—white footsteps in white snow in a whiteout are difficult to follow.

The weather tends to be better at full moon, and the equatorial moon is so strong that you do not need to use your headlamp when climbing by moonlight, from full moon to half moon.

GETTING TO THE PEAKS

How you get to the bottom of the route and how much support you want or need depends on you and the route you are attempting. An agency in the United States or Europe or from Quito can organize everything for you. If you want to go it alone by relying on public transport, then do it yourself—it is invariably cheaper but requires more time and some knowledge of Spanish.

Agencies

Many agencies in Quito offer guides, transport, and cooks, as much or as little as you want. English-, German-, and French-speaking guides are

Katanbatic cloud on Chimborazo

available, as well as guides who speak a number of other languages. If
you are paying for a cook and food, ask to see the menu to make sure
you like what you will be getting. If you just want transport, a jeep and
driver costs around US$140 a day or US$100 for a half-day.

The better agencies with mountain experience in Quito (international dialing code +593 2) include the following:

➡ **Altamontaña and Compañia de Guías de Montaña,** Jorge Washington 425 and 6 de Diciembre (tel/fax 504773), Apartado 17-21-
   1081, Quito, open Monday–Friday, *guiasdemontania@accessinter.net*

➡ **Andisimo Travel,** 9 de Octubre 479 and Roca (tel/fax 223030),
   open Monday–Friday, *www.andisimo.com*

➡ **Pamir Adventure Travel,** J. L. Mera 721 and Veintimilla (tel
   220892, fax 547576), Apartado 17-16-190, Quito, open Monday–
   Friday, *htorres@pi.pro.ec*

➡ **Safari,** Calama 380 and J. L. Mera (tel 552505, fax 223381),
   Apartado 17-11-6060, Quito, open every day, *admin@safari.com.ec*

➡ **Sierra Nevada,** Pinto 637 and Amazonas (tel 553658, fax
   554936), open Monday–Friday, *marlopez@pi.pro.ec*

➡ **Surtrek,** Amazonas 897 and Wilson (tel 561129, fax 561132),
   Apartado 17-03-604, Quito, open Monday–Friday,
   surtrek1@surtrek.com.ec

In Riobamba (international dialing code +593 3, within Ecuador 03),
the following agencies specialize in mountaineering:

➡ **Alta Montaña,** Borja 3517 and Diego de Ibarra (tel/fax
   940950), open Monday–Friday

➡ **Andes Trek,** Colón 2225 and 10 de Agosto (tel 940964, fax
   940963), open Monday–Friday, *andestrek@exploringecuador.com*

➡ **Expediciones Andes,** Argentinos 3860 and Zambrano (tel
   964915), open Monday–Friday

South American Explorers' Club

The most up-to-date noncommercial source of information on getting
around and getting things done in Ecuador is available from the South
American Explorers' Club, which has offices in Quito (Jorge Washington 311 and Leonidas Plaza, tel/fax 225228, *explorer@saec.org.ec*); Ithaca,
New York, United States; and Lima and Cuzco, Peru. Membership costs
US$40 a year for individuals/US$60 for couples. Services for members
include e-mail, *post restante,* luggage storage, and a library. Specific

mountaineering information depends on the experience of the volunteers working at the club at the time of your visit and the accuracy of those who have recently written trip reports.

The club also recommends the website *www.cotopaxi.com* run by Tim Tadder and Ray Marx, two U.S. Quito Colegio Americano teachers and climbers.

Guides

Any guide you hire should be a member of the Ecuadorian guides' association, ASEGUIM, which has acceptably high standards for its members. Eight ASEGUIM guides were trained intensively in Chamonix by French guides from ENSA for three months in 1994. These eight then formed the training section of ASEGUIM, and over a period of four years they have trained other guides. Two guides, Javier Herrera and Juan Espiñosa, have received further training in France and Bolivia, and they are working toward qualifying for international certification with the UIAGM.

Note: At the time of this writing, only one of the guides in Baños was an ASEGUIM member. Guiding and equipment organized in Baños can be of dangerously low quality.

Public Transport

A road is bad when the beasts tumble into mud-holes and disappear right out of sight.

Edward Whymper
Travels Amongst the Great Andes of the Equator (1892)

Ecuador is the most densely populated country in South America, and it shows in the abundant availability of cheap public transport. Buses link all the major settlements with Quito on an hourly to daily basis, with journeys costing about US$1 per hour.

If you plan on using buses, you will need protectors for your crampons and ice axe so that they can be carried safely. Rice/flour/sugar sacks available from markets make ideal rucksack protectors, and they make your sack look just like any other piece of luggage and not a gringo sack worth stealing.

Smaller settlements are linked to regional or local centers by regular pickup services. If you want to get to somewhere away from a settlement, like a hut or road head, then get to the closest sizable village and hire a pickup to take you. Be prepared to haggle with the driver. Directions are given in the "Access" section for each mountain.

Note: Strikes are a way of political life in Ecuador, and public transport is one of the first sectors to support a strike.

PARKS AND RESERVES

Entrance fees are mentioned in the text where appropriate. In general, entrance fees are US$10 per person or the sucre equivalent. Services and infrastructure in the protected areas vary from not a lot to nonexistent. Many people would like to know what happens to the US$10 every foreigner pays to enter the Cotopaxi National Park. It certainly isn't spent on providing services in the park.

HUTS

Off Belay (1980) carried an account of a night in the Ilinizas hut (15 beds): "With some effort we were comfortable with 22 inside. The arrival of 36 more, which made a total of 58, presented a serious space problem. We squeezed together as closely as possible and asked them to be quiet because we were getting up early to climb. But we were stuck among jokers, sick people, and storytellers. The singing, talking, and discourteous behaviour lasted until 4 A.M. We arose at 5 A.M."

Ecuador's first hut, the wooden octagonal-shaped Fabián Zurita hut at 4,500 m/14,750 ft on the Murallas Rojas route on Chimborazo, was opened in 1964. A year later the Nuevos Horizontes hut opened just below the saddle at the Ilinizas. The Cotopaxi hut opened in 1971, and the present road to the car park was finished in 1974. The hut was expanded in 1977 to accommodate a capacity of eighty people, but it is now a disgrace: there are insufficient bunks, stoves, and cooking and eating equipment; the toilets rarely function and this when it is the most popular hut in Ecuador and foreigners pay US$10 per night for the pleasure of staying there. If even half the money paid went into hut maintenance, it would be hugely better. The higher of Chimborazo's two huts (technically, the Whymper hut) was opened in 1980 at 5,000 m/16,400 ft to commemorate the first centenary of Whymper's climb. It is better than the Cotopaxi hut, but it suffers from an inadequate number of stoves and cooking equipment. In 1981 the Cayambe hut opened, but it too fell into disrepair—in 1990 the hut guardian prized up sections of the parquet floor to burn in order to keep warm. However, the hut was fully renovated in 1994 and is currently the best of Ecuador's huts.

Hut fees are around US$10 per person per night or the equivalent in sucres. The dollarization of Ecuador's currency may affect hut fees. In general, Ecuadorian huts are convenient but noisy and dirty. Camping is an increasingly popular option as a little extra weight guarantees you use of cooking equipment (your own) and a good night's sleep.

SECURITY

Ecuador is not as safe as it once was. You should be on guard at airports and bus terminals, in cities and tourist destinations, and whenever you travel by public transport. Once off the tourist circuit or in the mountains, however, you can relax.

If you arrive at the airport at night, take a yellow taxi from immediately outside the International Arrivals exit. This should not cost more than US$4 for the ride to the new town. Bus terminals and buses are frequented by thieves. Never leave anything unattended, keep in physical contact with your luggage at all times, do not use the luggage racks inside buses (theft), and do not put anything on the floor or under the seat (contortionist bag slashers). Bags given to the driver or helper (*ayudante*) to put on the roof are generally safe from theft, if not from dirt and rain. Do not travel by interprovincial bus at night.

In general, avoid the old town (*centro histórico*) in Quito; if you go, don't take anything you value (for example, your wallet, watch, or camera)—pickpocketing and mugging of tourists are common. Do not go up the Panecillo hill. Take all normal big city precautions while you are in the new town, especially in Amazonas. Do not walk in El Ejido or La Carolina parks, day or night. Be extra careful in the new town at night; buses stop running about 8 P.M., and the electric Trole stops at midnight. Take a taxi if you are going more than a few blocks.

Huts tend to be safe places in which to leave your kit while you climb, but don't take along anything of value that you are not going to carry up the mountain.

However far away from the crowd you feel, it is worth remembering that Ecuador is the most densely populated country in South America, and there are people all over the place. Do not leave camps below the snow line unattended—pack up your kit and hide it.

General strikes are often called, and the level of public support for strikes varies considerably from total to negligible. These actions are not directed against tourists, for whom the main problem is the inconvenience of not being able to get around. Not only does transport go on strike but demonstrators block roads in the cities while peasants block them in the countryside. This makes travel all but impossible until the end of the strike.

MAPS

The Ecuadorian Instituto Geográfico Militar (IGM) produces 1:50,000 and in some cases 1:25,000 and 1:100,000 maps to all mountains in the country. On the 1:50,000 maps, contours are generally at 40-m/130-ft intervals. Blue contours indicating permanent snow cover are grossly exaggerated. Later editions are often extensively updated, leading to path and road additions, name changes, and even contour changes.

To buy maps when you are in Ecuador, go to the IGM on Calle Telmo Paz y Miño (clearly visible from much of the city because of its planetarium) Monday through Thursday, 8:30 A.M. to 12:30 P.M. and 1 to 4 P.M., and Friday, 8:30 A.M. to 1 P.M. (tel 522066, 522148). You will need to leave your passport at the gate (copies are not accepted). Service can be slow, so be prepared to wait—especially if an original is not available and you need a photocopy. Maps and copies cost up to US$3 a sheet depending on the exchange rate and when prices were last adjusted.

A number of maps needed by climbers are restricted (reservado). To obtain a restricted map, you need to turn in a photocopy of your passport and to fill out the relevant forms at the IGM sales office. There can be a delay of up to two weeks in getting restricted maps.

The best selection of maps available outside Ecuador is from Omni Resources, 1004 South Mebane Street, Burlington, North Carolina, 27215, United States (tel 910 227 8300), and in the United Kingdom from Stanfords, 12-14 Long Acre, London WC2E 9LP (tel 0171 836 1321).

Ecuador-based Latin American Travel Consultants (LATC) can obtain any maps available in Ecuador and send them. Contact LATC, P.O. Box 17-17-908, Quito, Ecuador, lata@pi.pro.ec for more information.

ALTITUDE ILLNESS

Two forms of altitude sickness are fatal if unrecognized and untreated: High Altitude Pulmonary Edema (HAPE) and High Altitude Cerebral Edema (HACE).

Chimborazo's southeast side from El Altar

High Altitude Pulmonary Edema (HAPE). This condition occurs when the blood-gas barrier in the lungs starts breaking up owing to the difference in pressure between the pulmonary artery and the air inside the lungs. If untreated, the victim will drown. Symptoms include the need to sit upright in order to breathe, pink frothy sputum, blue lips, severe breathlessness, and gargling in the lungs.

Treatment is descent and nifedipine (a diuretic). Take 10mg sublingually (break open a capsule and hold it under the tongue), followed by 20mg (slow release) taken orally every 8 hours while descending. Take acetazolamide while descending.

High Altitude Cerebral Edema (HACE). This condition is caused by the brain swelling and becoming crushed against the skull. If untreated, HACE leads to brain hemorrhage, coma, and death. Symptoms include severe headache, vomiting, loss of balance, disorientation, vision problems, incoherent speech, behavioral changes, and coma.

Treatment is descent and dexamethasone (Decadron), a steroid that works directly to reduce the swelling of the brain. If the victim is in a coma, an injection of 8g dexamethasone phosphate in the upper outer quadrant of the buttock is required. For a debilitating headache, take 2mg pills; take four pills immediately in an emergency, then continue to take one pill four times a day while descending to a lower altitude.

In the case of HAPE or HACE, if the symptoms are severe, the victim should be taken down immediately even if it is the middle of the night. Deterioration can be rapid, victims can die in just a few hours, and it is easier to help an ill person walk than to carry an unconscious body.

Although HAPE and HACE are extremely rare below 3,000 m/10,000 ft, they are still possible. All members of the group should be aware of the symptoms and appropriate treatments.

SLEEP DISTURBANCE

The biggest source of sleep disturbance for climbers in Ecuador is the noise made by other people in the huts. Apart from this problem, an altitude factor (not entirely understood) causes periodic (Cheyne-Stokes) breathing, a condition in which the sleeper stops breathing every cycle. At sea level, this is serious and will land you in a hospital. At high altitude, it is merely worrisome for those who are close enough to hear because they initially think that the person has died. The quality of sleep at high altitude is poor, with more arousals and less rapid eye movement (REM) sleep. The arousals lead to people waking up while in the middle of a dream; hence, dreams often appear more vivid than at sea level.

SUN PROTECTION

The affection that is termed 'snow-blindness' is inflammation of the eyes. They become extraordinarily sensitive to light. The lids refuse to open; tears come freely, and coagulating round the lashes glue the lids fast. To apply lotion effectively, the lids must be forced open, and the instant this is done the patient will imagine that red-hot needles are being driven through the eyes into the brain. The pain is acute, and sometimes makes strong men howl.

Edward Whymper
Travels Amongst the Great Andes of the Equator (1892)

Ultraviolet (UV) light at high altitude on or near the equator is extraordinarily strong. Without proper eye protection, it is possible to get snow blindness after as little as 15 minutes above 5,000 m/16,000 ft. It does not matter whether the day is sunny or cloudy, in fact more UV light is reflected on cloudy days.

Snow blindness is not normally apparent until the night after the damage has been done. The pain has been described as what it must be like to have acid or boiling water poured into your eyes. The next day, the victim often cannot see and will have to be led down the mountain. Amethocaine eyedrops help relieve the pain, but this remedy comes a bit late: snow blindness causes permanent eye injury—part of the retina is burnt out—which means victims are more susceptible in the future. Wear sunglasses that provide 100 percent protection against UV light. Ski goggles with 100 percent-UV-protection lenses are useful for cloudy days, bad weather, and as spares in case you break or lose your glacier glasses.

Sunburn is a serious business at high altitude and can happen on completely overcast days. The power of the equatorial sun reflecting off snow will burn the skin under the chin, up the nostrils, and behind the ears.

The best protection is to keep all your skin covered—a hat or helmet is essential to avoid sunstroke, and a noseguard that clips to your sunglasses saves getting suntan lotion all over your glasses.

FOOD POISONING, WATER TREATMENT, AND GIARDIASIS

After acclimatization, the most common mountain health problem is a bout with food poisoning that was picked up in Quito. A course of antibiotics, such as ciprofloxacin, and oral rehydration salts should cure this quickly and allow ascent to continue.

Water supplies to huts are from clean glacier-melt water, but storage conditions are often less than hygienic, so all water should be boiled. Boiling for one minute is sufficient to kill anything that can live at the altitude where you happen to be.

It is possible to contract giardiasis anywhere there are animals, and llamas are quite happy up to 5,000 m/16,000 ft. The main indicator of giardiasis is diarrhea together with a huge and painful buildup of gas in the stomach and intestines that leads to "farting through your mouth." Use iodine-based water purification tablets or tincture or a filter pump to treat all your water while out in the country. If you get giardiasis, take tinidazole antibiotics.

ACCIDENTS AND RESCUE

Climbing in Ecuador appears at first sight to be pretty safe. However, it is worth remembering that during the 1990s there were two big accidents. On November 10, 1993, two roped parties descending the Normal Route on Chimborazo met one roped party ascending below the Veintemilla summit. The slope avalanched, sweeping six French, two Ecuadorians, a Chilean, and a Swiss into a crevasse at 5,700 m/18,700 ft where they were buried and died. On Easter Sunday, 1996, fourteen daytrippers were killed when an avalanche reached the hut on Cotopaxi.

Because of the power of the equatorial sun, you should plan to be on the summit within a couple of hours of dawn and then head down shortly afterward, aiming to be off the glaciers well before midday to avoid avalanche danger.

In case of accident, the normal routes are popular, so there is a chance of help. But the mountains are so big that help might be some time in coming. In the case of the Chimborazo disaster, other parties on the same route were unaware of the avalanche. The Cotopaxi, Chimborazo, and Cayambe huts are permanently staffed and have radios, but remember that the guardians rarely speak English. Outside the normal routes on the popular mountains, an accident will have to be dealt with by the climbers involved with no expectation of outside help until someone descends, gets to a telephone, and calls out the cavalry. Always start with the agency that organized your trip or transport, followed by your embassy or consulate.

The Ecuadorian guides' association, ASEGUIM, has experience in rescue (and more in body recovery). If you are climbing with an ASEGUIM guide, rescue is free, you just pay expenses; otherwise, it costs upward of US$1,000 a day with an up-front deposit of US$3,000 before anyone will go and look for you if you are uninsured. Although health care in many hospitals in Quito is good, most people prefer to be treated at home by doctors sharing the same first language. Medical repatriation is extremely expensive, and so insurance is again recommended.

Note: Solo climbing on glaciers is a lethal pastime in Ecuador as elsewhere. If you are determined to climb in this way, you should carry your passport (preferably in your rucksack and not on your person) so those unfortunate enough to find your body can identify it quickly and easily.

ENVIRONMENTAL IMPACT

Litter is in evidence on the normal routes and around the huts owing to the number of people climbing, as well as local daytrippers. You should be careful not to add to the problem. All trash should be carried out to the nearest big town (for example, Quito or Riobamba). If you can carry your packets, tins, and other rubbish up the mountain, there is no reason why you can't carry them down. Toilet paper should be burnt and feces buried.

Trash cans in national parks, especially in Cotopaxi, are only infrequently emptied. It is better to take your rubbish back out of the park rather than use the cans. Similarly, it doesn't hurt to carry out your rubbish from the huts.

To some extent the Ecuadorian government recognizes the economic importance of tourism. The protected area system, made up of reserves and parks, is reasonably extensive. But the more important that tourism is shown to be, the more care will be taken on a macro scale of the incredible natural diversity of the country. Perhaps someone will try to sort out Quito's air pollution problem, and one day, before all available land is covered in ugly plastic greenhouses and windbreaks for roses, attempts will be made to control flower production, which spread like a blight in the late 1990s.

HOW TO USE THIS BOOK

Prices are quoted in U.S. dollars. This is appropriate because Ecuador began moving toward using the U.S. dollar as its primary currency in March of 2000.

Mountains are listed in order of location from north to south, first those to the west of the Sierra, from Chiles to Chimborazo (including Mojanda, although technically it is in the Interandean region) then those to the east of the Sierra, from Imbabura to Sangay (including Imbabura and Rumiñahui, also in the Interandean region).

The approach route is shown on a map for each mountain. Topo photographs with marked route lines are included where available. For each mountain and route described, the following information is given.

Alternative names. Where relevant, alternative names or spellings are given in parentheses following the most commonly used name for the mountain. These names or spellings might be found in older descriptions of mountaineering in Ecuador.

Heights. Heights given are the most accurate known and come from a variety of sources, mainly from the IGM. All Ecuadorian maps are metric only. To convert meters to feet, multiply by 3.2808. (Or for a reasonably accurate estimate, multiply by 3 and add 10 percent.) To convert feet to meters, divide by 3.2808.

First known/recorded ascent of mountain and/or route. The most complete information possible is given—ideally the month, day, year, and the first and last names of the first ascenders (in alphabetical order) plus their nationalities. Omissions are owing to a lack of information.

Maps. The best available 1:50,000 IGM sheet needed for the approach and access is given. If two or more IGM maps are listed, it means that two or more maps are needed to cover the mountain.

Access. The best route by public and private transportation to the start of the approach is described, as well as other options when relevant.

Approach. The best walk-in to a hut, basecamp, or the start of the route is described.

Routes. A selection of routes is described for each major peak, although other routes might have been climbed and still others might be waiting to be climbed. Route descriptions should be considered with the following caveat in mind: significant seasonal changes in snow and ice cover occur, glaciers move, and El Niño affects weather patterns every three to seven years on average—badly every fifteen to twenty years. This means that the exact line of a route changes, and entire routes come in and go out of condition.

Grade. Two sets of grades are given for each climb: one for North American readers and one for Europeans.

The first set is a U.S. alpine grade for snow/ice routes using a Yosemite Decimal System grade in parentheses for rock pitches when relevant.

The second grade is a French alpine grade followed by a Union International des Associations d'Alpinisme rock grade in parentheses when relevant.

The U.S. system is based on the Welzenbach scale, which rates routes from Grade I to Grade VI. Grade I is used for routes up to 50° snow or 35° ice, and the grades get progressively harder up until Grade VI, which is used to classify routes with very thin or technical 90° ice.

The French Alpine System is similar, but it uses words abbreviated to letters instead of numerals. It starts at F for *Facil* and proceeds through PD (*Peu Difficile*—a little difficult), AD (*Assez Difficile*—fairly difficult),

D (*Difficile*—difficult), TD (*Très Difficile*—very difficult), and ED (*Extrêmement Difficile*—extremely difficult).

The overall grade of the route takes into account technical difficulty, the difficulty of the hardest section of the route, exposure, commitment, and so forth. However, it is important to remember that most routes start higher in elevation than the point where most North American and European mountains end, so acclimatization is more important than technical ability.

Maximum slope. The approximate angle of the steepest section of the route is given. This is steeper than the average slope of the route, but it shows the maximum difficulty.

Elevation gain. Vertical altitude gain is estimated from the logical start of the route where the climbing begins—normally from the start of the glacier or from the hut.

Time required. An approximate timing is based on a fit and acclimatized person climbing in good to average conditions.

chiles

4,723 m/15,495 ft

NOVEMBER 27, 1869, WILHELM REISS AND ALPHONS STÜBEL (GERMANY) FROM COLOMBIA

Maps: Tufiño (restricted; the 1:100,000 Tulcán is unrestricted)

This is a good acclimatization peak made up of—unusual for Ecuador—good rock. Chiles is way up north and part of the border between Ecuador and Colombia. As a result, few people climb it. If you want to avoid the crowds, Chiles is ideal.

The volcano is a caldera 2 km/1.25 mi wide, open to the north. It's considered active and so is permanently monitored—you will notice a definite smell of sulfur at times during the climb. The smoking volcano you can see to the north of Chiles is Cumbal in Colombia.

The landscape around Chiles is bizarre—*frailejones,* many more than 2 m/6½ ft high (and some double that height), stand watch for miles and miles in the *páramo* El Angel. The journey by road to the north takes you through a landscape very different from the rest of the Ecuadorian Sierra. It is all very green. Out of Ibarra there are steep-sided, heavily vegetated valleys. You also pass through the Chota valley, the center of Ecuador's highland black population, where people traditionally carry loads on their heads rather than on their backs.

ACCESS

From Quito's Terminal Terrestre take a bus to Tulcán (5½ hours, US$3). Four companies operate buses on the route, and the buses leave about every 15 minutes.

From the Tulcán terminal, take a taxi (5 minutes, US$0.75) to the stop where buses leave for Maldonado and Tufiño, opposite the Colegio Nacional Tulcán. One bus per day leaves for Maldonado around midday. Buses leave every couple of hours for Tufiño (1 hour, US$0.50). Ideally, take the Maldonado bus to a spot where the road reaches its highest point above and beyond Lagunas Verdes, about 1 hour beyond

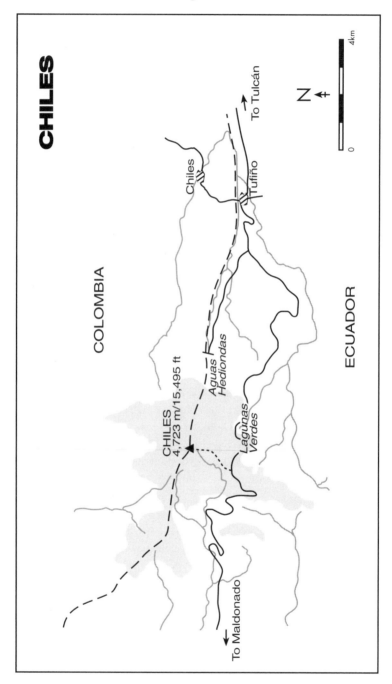

CHILES

COLOMBIA

Chiles

Tufiño

To Tulcán

CHILES
4,723 m/15,495 ft

Aguas
Hediondas

Lagunas
Verdes

To Maldonado

ECUADOR

N

0 4km

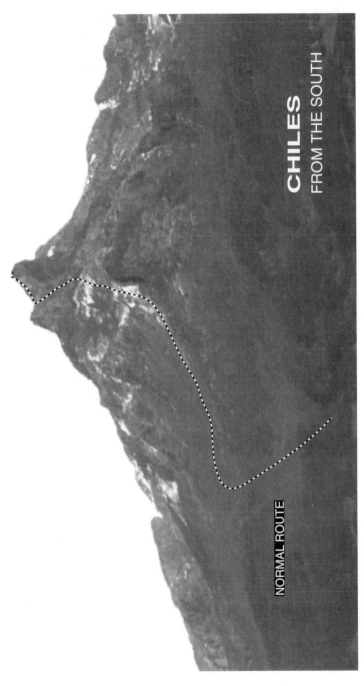

CHILES
FROM THE SOUTH

NORMAL ROUTE

Tufiño. If you don't catch the Maldonado bus and don't want to spend the night in Tulcán, take the bus to Tufiño and either organize transport in the village or walk. There are occasional camionetas going to Maldonado but not enough traffic to make hitchhiking a definite proposition. There is nowhere to stay in Tufiño, although there are some basic shops and places to eat. The typical climate is illustrated by the region's most popular item of clothing—a heavy wool poncho.

Note: Carry your passport—there is a military checkpoint before Tufiño.

APPROACH

From Tufiño it takes about 5 hours to walk to the highest point on the road before it starts dropping toward Maldonado and the coast. In Tufiño, follow the main cobbled road up, ignore the left turn in the village, and follow the road to the thermals of Aguas Hediondas (literally, "the stinking waters"). The stench of sulfur is strong. If you do decide

Frailejones near Chiles

to bathe, use the developed pools and do not follow the waters uphill—a number of people have been overcome by the fumes and died. A safer set of cool thermals where it is also possible to camp are reached before the turnoff to Aguas Hediondas by leaving the road on the first sharp right turn out of Tufiño and dropping down left.

After about 3 hours of walking from Tufiño you reach Lagunas Verdes (where it is possible to camp), and the road reaches a high point with a sign above the road to the left. It is possible to climb from here, but it is steeper. After a short descent, the road then rises again. The highest point is 1 hour farther on at the site of a small concrete hut above the road to the left.

From the high point on the road, head up right to join the ridge. Following it to the top takes 3 hours, crossing good rock. When you enter the crater near the top, you will find scree followed by a short ridge scramble to reach the summit. Camping is possible ½ hour above the road, to the right of the ridge.

Descent: Same; 1 hour from the summit to the road.

cotacachi (cotocachi)

4,939 m/16,204 ft

APRIL 24, 1880, JEAN ANTOINE AND LOUIS CARREL (ITALY) AND EDWARD WHYMPER (U.K.)

Maps: Imantag, Otavalo

Dominating the area around the market town of Otavalo, Cotacachi is Ecuador's eleventh highest peak. At its base is the ancient and beautiful lake-filled caldera of Cuicocha. When Edward Whymper climbed Cotacachi, it had a sizeable glacier, and until the 1970s, people used to go up to the glacier to cut ice, wrap it in grass, and use mules to carry it down to Otavalo to make refreshing drinks for the Saturday market. Now the glacier has gone, and the mountain continues to suffer from heavy erosion. Whatever route you take, it is necessary to climb steep and loose rock. Rockfall is a real danger—wear a helmet.

According to some, the name comes from the words *cota* (tower) and *cachi* (high mountain). Others say the name comes from the Quichua words *gacha* (lake) and *kachi* (salt) leading to the name Mount Saltlake. Legend has it that Cotacachi was the wife of Imbabura.

Whymper was impressed by the nature of the country surrounding Cotacachi and wrote: "The lower slopes of our mountain, and the comparatively flat ground at its base, were rent and riven in a most extreme manner. In no other part of Ecuador is there anything equaling this extraordinary assemblage of fissures, intersecting one another irregularly and forming a perfect maze of impassable clefts. The general appearance of the country between the villages of Cotocachi and Otavalo is not very unlike that of a biscuit which has been smashed by a blow of a fist. The cracks are all V-shaped, and though seldom of great breadth are often very profound" (*Travels,* 1892).

Whymper was also impressed by the weather on Cotacachi—he got hit by a storm, which, for the only time during his whole trip, prevented

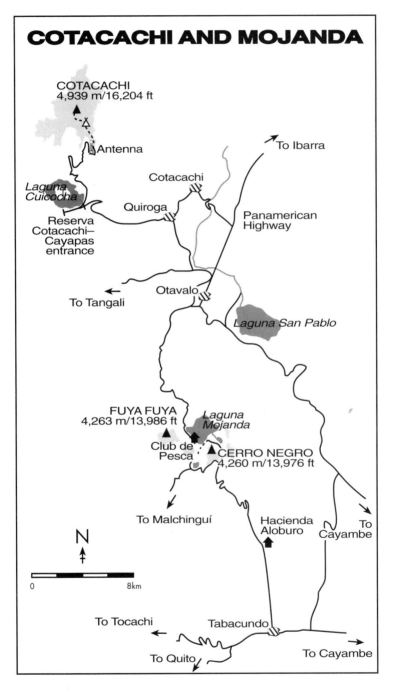

COTACACHI AND MOJANDA

COTACACHI
4,939 m/16,204 ft

Antenna

Cotacachi

Laguna Cuicocha

Quiroga

To Ibarra

Panamerican Highway

Reserva Cotacachi–Cayapas entrance

To Tangali

Otavalo

Laguna San Pablo

FUYA FUYA
4,263 m/13,986 ft

Laguna Mojanda

Club de Pesca

CERRO NEGRO
4,260 m/13,976 ft

To Malchinguí

Hacienda Aloburo

To Cayambe

N

0   8km

To Tocachi

Tabacundo

To Quito

To Cayambe

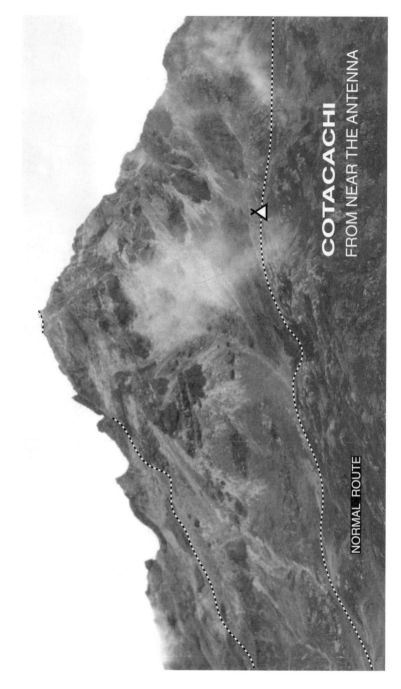

COTACACHI
FROM NEAR THE ANTENNA

NORMAL ROUTE

him from erecting his tent properly. People have also been struck by lightning.

Note: There is no reliable water source on the mountain—take all you need.

ACCESS

From Quito's Terminal Terrestre, take a bus to Otavalo (2 hours, US$2). In Otavalo, go to the junction of Calle 31 de Octubre with Calle Calderon and take a bus to Quiroga (25 minutes, US$0.20). In Quiroga, hire a pickup to *la antennae* or *los torres de transmisión* (1 hour, US$12). The route goes to the Reserva Cotacachi–Cayapas entrance (open 8:30 A.M. to 5 P.M. daily, no charge) where you must hand in your passport if you are going to spend the night in the park. You must also get the park guardian to unlock the cable barrier to the road to the antenna, which is the right turn immediately after the park entrance building.

It is possible to hire a jeep from Quito (US$100 for up to four people, US$25 for each additional person up to nine) or a pickup in Otavalo to take you to *la antennae.* You can walk from Otavalo if you've got a spare couple of days, although this involves a lot of road slogging as does walking from Quiroga. The walk from Laguna Cuicocha to the antenna is far more pleasant, but it involves 1,000 m/3,300 ft of ascent and takes 4 to 5 hours.

APPROACH

From the last hairpin bend before the highest antenna, head off right following the path along the grassy ridge. After 1 hour you reach a flat though exposed and waterless camping spot on the ridge. Follow the path left across an intermittent stream and head up to reach better but still waterless camping before a saddle after another 30 minutes.

NORMAL ROUTE

Grade (5.5)/(IV), 70°, 300 m/1,000 ft, 3 hours from camp

From the saddle, follow the cairn-marked path down and then traverse left before rising and going up and through the first col, staying on the right. After the col, a yellow scree slope goes up right. Follow it to a flat spot below where the scree ends and the rock becomes steeper and more solid. Rope up and climb the gully (10 m/30 ft of 5.5/IV) before traversing out right to a belay (15 m/50 ft). Scramble diagonally up left back to the gully, enter it, and then follow it up to the summit (50 m/165 ft).

Descent: Rappel 25 m/80 ft from below the summit back into the gully. Rappel 50 m/165 ft straight down the gully to arrive at the start of the climbing. From here, the descent to camp is the same (1½ hours). From camp, it takes 1 hour to the road.

If you are walking out, there is no need to follow the road back down to the park entrance. It is more interesting to follow the ridge to the right (east) of the antenna ridge and then drop down right to join the road 15 minutes from where the crater path joins from the right. The Cuicocha crater is 3 km/1.75 mi across, is filled with a lake, has two volcanic dome islands, and is well worth a visit.

CHAPTER 5

mojanda

Mojanda is a huge blown-out caldera that measures 2.8 km/1.75 mi east-west and 2.2 km/1.3 mi north-south—the base of the mountain is 20 km/12.5 mi across. Edward Whymper commented that Mojanda "perhaps covers a greater space than any other mountain in Ecuador" (*Travels,* 1892). The two principal peaks—Fuya Fuya and Cerro Negro—are 3.75 km/2.3 mi apart, and both make good acclimatization climbs. Three beautiful lakes adorn the route as well.

On October 30 each year hundreds of people walk the old road from Quito over Mojanda arriving in Otavalo the next day in an event named "Mojanda Arriba." The peaks can be popular at weekends—go midweek to avoid the crowds.

A dirt road links the bases of the two peaks, making the journey from Tabacundo to Otavalo (or vice versa) over the mountain possible. However, this route is only passable by vehicle in the driest of conditions. Just a little rain and the mud becomes impossibly greasy. However, it is still possible to walk and make both ascents on one trip. If you plan to do this, logistically it makes sense to start in Otavalo, hire a pickup to Laguna Mojanda, climb Fuya Fuya, follow the dirt road around to Cerro Negro, climb that peak, and then descend to Tabacundo.

FUYA FUYA

4,263 m/13,986 ft
Maps: Mojanda, Otavalo

Fuya Fuya is climbed from the inside of the Mojanda crater. The largest of Mojanda's three crater lakes lies below, backed by the rock pinnacles of Cerro Negro.

Access

(See the Cotacachi and Mojanda map.)

CERRO NEGRO

FROM THE ROAD TO THE SOUTH

NORMAL ROUTE

The tourist mecca of Otavalo is the starting point for most ascents of Fuya Fuya. Buses from Quito's Terminal Terrestre leave frequently every day heading to Otavalo (2 hours, US$2).

Approach

It is 15 cobbled kilometers (9 mi) and 1,200 vertical meters (4,000 ft) from Otavalo's main square (not the Plaza de Ponchos) to Laguna Mojanda. With the map and careful reading, you could work out a route up avoiding the cobbles. If not, hire a pickup in Otavalo to take you to Laguna Mojanda (less than 1 hour, US$12).

From the main square, follow Calle Sucre south. It bears left and crosses straight over the Panamerican Highway next to the concrete footbridge with the foot section missing. A few meters/yards on, the road forks. Take the left fork (the street is called Valle del Tambo) and continue all the way to the derelict Club de Pesca hut on the shore of Laguna Mojanda at 3,750 m/12,200 ft.

Do not walk down the cobbles back to Otavalo unless you want to cripple yourself. (Thus spake the voice of experience.)

NORMAL ROUTE

Note: There is no water on this route after Laguna Mojanda.

With your back to the Club de Pesca, Fuya Fuya is the highest point in front and to the left. Follow any one of the numerous paths over the two *zanja* ditches. The paths then start joining up. Head for the path going straight up onto the ridge. At the ridge, turn left and continue.

Stay left (south) of the principal ridge until you are below the col between the subsidiary (right) and main (left) summits. Head straight up to the col, turn left, and continue to the main summit.

It takes 1½ hours to reach the summit from the lake.

Descent: Same, in half the time.

CERRO NEGRO

4,260 m/13,976 ft

Maps: Cayambe, Mojanda

This good acclimatization peak features spectacular views on the way up and from the summit. On a good day you can see Cayambe and the valley below it, the Pichinchas with Quito perched on a shelf below, as well as the Sierra and the other mountains stretching south.

Note: There is no water on this route and none available beyond the rainwater collector just above Hacienda Aloburo.

Access

(See the Cotacachi and Mojanda map.)

Go in via the town of Tabacundo on the Panamerican Highway. Take an Otavalo bus from Quito's Terminal Terrestre and get off at Tabacundo (1½ hours, US$1.50).

You could hire a pickup in Tabacundo to take you as high up the road as it can get, which varies depending on the pickup, the driver, and the road conditions.

A jeep from Quito costs US$80 and takes 1½ hours to reach the last turning point at the farm buildings 7 km/4.5 mi from Tabacundo.

Approach

It is 13 km/8 mi from Tabacundo to the bottom of the route. From the main square in Tabacundo facing the church, exit on the bottom left corner, go one block west, and then turn right (north) and head up the dirt road where there is a sign that says "Lagunas de Mojanda." The road continues past the ubiquitous greenhouses of the area, with Cerro Negro visible at the head of the valley and Cayambe and the valley of the town of the same name behind.

If you are walking, you want to get on the ridge to the left that runs east of the mountain. The easiest way to do this is to follow the road until you reach the point where it cuts back left 5 km/3 mi from Tabacundo and a track continues straight on. Follow the track for a few hundred meters/yards until you reach its end and then cut back to the left following cow paths. Follow these up to the ridge where there is a path through the *páramo.*

After 7 km/4.5 mi there are some farm buildings down left from the road. Unless it is dry and you are in a four-wheel-drive vehicle, you are unlikely to get farther in a vehicle.

Continue along the road to a fork just southeast of the mountain at about 3,870 m/12,700 ft. (The ridge path rejoins the road at this point.) Take the left fork, which drops slightly and goes along the base of the mountain. Continue until you are directly below the large rock face at about 3,685 m/12,090 ft.

NORMAL ROUTE

Although the path through the *páramo* is clearly visible above, the first few meters (yards) from the road are unclear. Thrash around until you reach the visible part of the path and follow it.

When it looks like you have to make a routefinding decision, go left. The path looks like it is going to get impossibly steep, but it doesn't.

It takes an hour to reach the summit from the road.

Descent: Same, in half the time.

guagua pichincha

4,794 m/15,728 ft

JULY 29, 1582, ALONSO DE AGUILAR, JUAN DE GALARZA, JUAN DE LONDOÑO, JOSÉ
TORIBIO DE ORTIGUERA, JUAN SÁNCHEZ, AND FRANCISCO DE UNCIBAY (SPAIN)

Map: Quito

Easy access from Quito through the beautiful valley of Lloa makes Guagua Pichincha a good acclimatization climb. Allegedly, Pichincha is a Colorado word meaning *pi* (water), *chin* (to cry), *cha* (of), *chani* (good) and therefore means "the good that cries."

Guagua (Quichua for "baby") is one of three major peaks that make up the Pichincha massif. The other two peaks are Padre Encantado and to the north the extinct Rucu ("Old") Pichincha. Quito is built on a shelf on the eastern side of the massif.

Warning: On no account try to climb Rucu Pichincha alone or in a group—the incidence of robbery (including armed), assault, and rape is far too high to justify the trip.

Guagua Pichincha's biggest recent explosion was in October 1999, when it sprinkled 2 mm of ash over the city (in contrast to the eruption in 1660 when it dumped 40 cm/15 in of ash on Quito and left the city in darkness for 4 days). A marked increase in activity had begun in 1997, with the volcano registering one to two explosions a month. In 1998 Quito was put on Yellow Alert because of intense seismic activity and a number of vapor explosions. Orange Alert was then declared in some adjacent areas in October 1999. The western side of the caldera has been eroded away, and vulcanologists believe—as do the inhabitants of Quito—that any major activity will be directed westward.

Note: At this time, access even to the village of Lloa is restricted to vulcanologists and other specialists. If you want to visit, check with authorities or agencies on arrival. The Spanish-language website *www.geofisico.cybw.net/volcan* is updated daily.

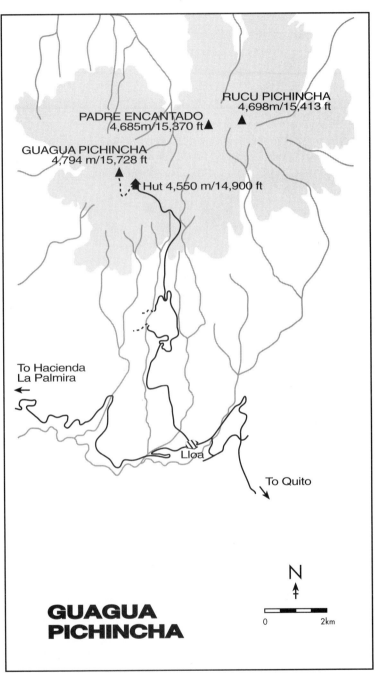

RUCU PICHINCHA
4,698m/15,413 ft

PADRE ENCANTADO
4,685m/15,370 ft▲

GUAGUA PICHINCHA
4,794 m/15,728 ft

▲ Hut 4,550 m/14,900 ft

To Hacienda
La Palmira

Lloa

To Quito

N

GUAGUA
PICHINCHA

0   2km

The active crater of Guagua Pichincha

ACCESS

Note: Do not attempt to enter this area without first checking the status in Quito.

A jeep from Quito via Lloa to a parking area at 4,150 m/13,600 ft takes 2½ hours and costs US$80 for up to four people, US$20 for each additional person up to nine. It is possible to go higher, but you need dry conditions and a four-wheel-drive vehicle.

Public transport is possible to Lloa at 3,030 m/9,940 ft—but tricky— and it leaves you with 1,750 m/5,750 ft of vertical ascent to the summit. Take the Trole electric bus to the southern end of the line and then a Popular local bus to Mena Dos. From this point, jump a bus or taxi to Lloa.

APPROACH

From the parking area, the track continues up (with a number of paths cutting corners) in 1 hour to the basic and often-staffed hut run by

Ecuadorian Civil Defense at 4,550 m/14,900 ft (US$2 per person, per night; take a sleeping bag, food, and stove).

NORMAL ROUTE

As Edward Whymper wrote: "Nothing more need be said about the ascent than that it might be made alone, by any moderately active lad" (*Travels,* 1892). Follow the broad path that rises diagonally left from behind the hut and goes up to the crater rim (10 minutes). Turn right and follow the ridge with great views down into the crater and fumaroles belching out sulfur gas. Stay slightly to the right to reach the first summit, which is marked by a concrete trig point. Continue along the ridge, down-climbing 3 m/10 ft below the first summit, and then continue on the ridge and scramble up 5 m/16 ft (the scramble is easier on the left side) to reach the true summit (35 minutes).

Descent: Down-climb back to the start of the final scramble and then descend left following the scree path well below the crater rim back to the hut (20 minutes).

ilinizas

Map: Machachi

Two mountains make up Ilinizas: one hard and icy, the other rocky and a lot easier. Iliniza Sur is a challenging mountain whatever way you climb it; Iliniza Norte is an excellent acclimatization peak.

The two mountains were called Iliniza and Tioniza, Male Mountain and Female Mountain. Legend has it that a young man from the coast arrived in Machachi on business and fell in love with a local girl. The girl's father had other plans for his daughter, however, and sought out the good services of a wizard to get rid of the unfortunate lover. The wizard turned the young suitor into Iliniza Sur. The daughter was distraught and wandered up and down the country telling her sorry tale until she came across the wizard, who granted her wish to be once again with her lover—he turned her into Iliniza Norte.

Note: The Ilinizas are now within a reserve. This will involve creating entrances and entrance charges.

ACCESS

It is possible to organize transport to get from Quito to La Virgen 4,240 m/ 13,910 ft in 2 hours. In dry conditions with a four-wheel-drive vehicle and a driver who knows how to drive it, you can get another 30 minutes higher, to the ridge before the moraine ridge. Jeep hire from Quito is US$100 for up to four people, US$20 for each additional person up to nine.

Alternatively, take a bus to Machachi from Quito (50 minutes, US$0.40). Buses do not leave from the Terminal Terrestre but from a side street near the southern Trole terminal. From Machachi's main square, walk up Avenida Amazonas for a couple of blocks to where pickups and the buses to El Chaupi are parked. Either arrange a pickup to La Virgen (2 hours, US$15) or take a bus to El Chaupi (45 minutes, US$0.60). From El Chaupi it is possible to walk to the Ilinizas hut via La Virgen and Hacienda El Refugio.

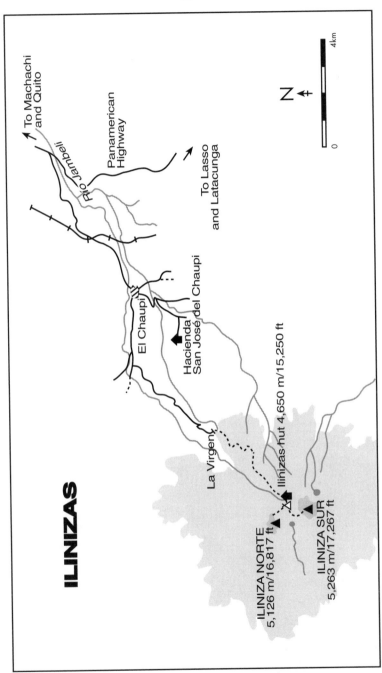

ILINIZAS

To Machachi
and Quito

Río Jambelí

Panamerican
Highway

To Lasso
and Latacunga

El Chaupi

Hacienda
San José del Chaupi

La Virgen

Ilinizas hut 4,650 m/15,250 ft

ILINIZA NORTE
5,126 m/16,817 ft

ILINIZA SUR
5,263 m/17,267 ft

N

0   4km

The second most comfortable way up to the Ilinizas is to get a horse to carry your kit. Just outside the village of El Chaupi is Hacienda San José del Chaupi where you can hire horses (US$15 per horse, each horse can carry three rucksacks). Call Rodrigo (tel 09 713986), who speaks English. It is also possible to spend the night at the hacienda (US$10 per person, which includes breakfast and gives you kitchen access).

APPROACH

From Hacienda San José del Chaupi: Follow the horses. If you lose sight of them, the route is as follows: head up the lane to the T-junction and turn left. Follow the lane and then take the second lane on the right, which ends in a field. At the far right corner of the field is a barbed wire and wood gate. Go through the gate, cross a ditch, and come out into an alpine meadow. Cross the meadow heading diagonally left. If you go too far left you will come to a barbed wire fence—follow this up. If you

Ilinizas Sur and Norte

go too far right you will come to a grass track—follow this leftward. The fence and grass track meet 1 hour from Hacienda San José del Chaupi.

Follow the path through more meadow heading for the center of a low hill on the skyline with bushes on it. Go through a barbed wire and wood gate and then head straight up to reach a path that goes diagonally up left to reach a track. Follow the track right. The track drops down to a stream crossing and meets another track at La Virgen, after another hour.

From La Virgen, follow the deeply rutted track up and through a Quinua wood. The track ends at the base of the moraine ridge where a path continues. Follow the ridge up until the angle flattens and you can see the orange hut off to the right. Follow the path to the hut, 1½ hours from La Virgen.

The small, staffed Ilinizas hut (fewer than 15 bunks) is at 4,650 m/ 15,250 ft and costs US$10 per person per night. To book a bunk, call Wladimir and Patricia Gallo (tel 09 440945). If there are more than a couple of other people in the hut, it is more comfortable to camp near the base of the glacier 45 minutes beyond the hut and 100 m/330 ft higher.

ILINIZA NORTE

5,126 m/16,817 ft

MAY 3, 1912, FRANZ HITI (AUSTRIA), NICOLÁS MARTÍNEZ, AND ALEJANDRO VILLAVICENCIO (ECUADOR)

Although it looks like a horrendous pile of scree, the rock on Iliniza Norte is pretty good by Ecuadorian standards, as long as you stay on the route. If you really want to torture yourself, try going straight up the south face as was done by Vincent and Grace Hoeman (U.S.) on January 14, 1968.

NORMAL ROUTE

Grade (5.3)/(II), 70°, 475 m/1,560 ft, 3 hours

From the hut, follow the path to the saddle. Cross the saddle and pick one of the paths that lead to the ridge on the right. To avoid too much scree bashing, join the ridge sooner rather than later. Follow the ridge until you reach a tower. At the tower, go right, drop down, and go around it. Traverse El Paso de la Muerte (the original name given by Martínez was El Desfiladero de la Muerte, "the gorge of death") to

NORMAL ROUTE

ILINIZA NORTE
FROM ILINIZA SUR

reach the bottom of a number of gullies where easy scrambling (5.3/II) takes you to the summit.

Warning: The traverse can be covered in ice and/or snow, especially in December and January. If this is the case, you will need crampons, ice ax, rope, and protection in order to be able to cross it safely.

Descent: Same

NORTH FACE ROUTE

Grade (5.3)/(II), 70°, 900 m/3,000 ft from La Virgen, 4½ hours

If you are not going to the hut, it makes sense to follow this route. From the base of the moraine ridge, head right to join the obvious path rising diagonally up across the orange scree. The path joins the Normal Route after El Paso de la Muerte and shortly before the north ridge.

Descent: Same or Normal Route

ILINIZA SUR

5,263 m/17,267 ft

MAY 4, 1880, JEAN ANTOINE AND LOUIS CARREL (ITALY)

This peak offers the most accessible hard climbing in the country. Edward Whymper was beaten twice by the peculiar mushroom cornice *(hongo)* that can form around the entire summit. His guides, the cousins Carrel, claimed to have climbed it from the north.

The mountain is suffering from glacial retreat, and the base of the glacier is pitted with rock that has fallen from above. Beware.

Approach

From the hut, follow the path up. At the fork, go left (right goes to Iliniza Norte) and continue to the glacier (45 minutes).

NORMAL ROUTE

Grade IV-/AD+, 70°, 600 m/2,000 ft, 4 hours

Follow the moraine above the glacier until you are beyond the La Rampa couloir and then drop to the glacier. Traverse right and then head up to reach a point to the right of a rock outcrop and head up. In dry conditions, this can be hard ice-gravel at 45°. The slope slackens above and trends rightward to a rightward traverse that brings you to a large crevasse. Depending

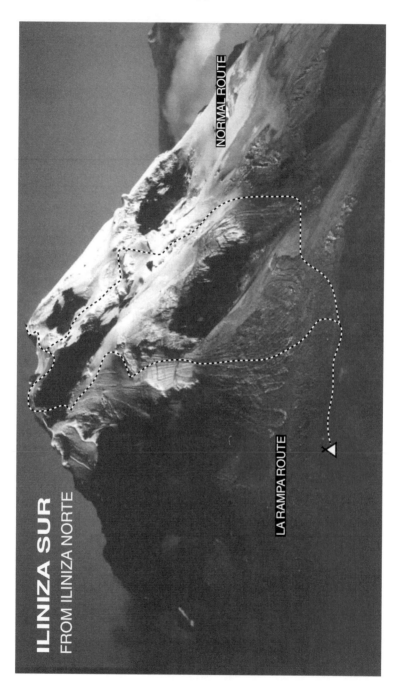

NORMAL ROUTE

LA RAMPA ROUTE

ILINIZA SUR
FROM ILINIZA NORTE

Moving through a major crevasse on the Normal Route, Iliniza Sur

on conditions, either cross the crevasse or cut back left into it and then climb out (3 m/10 ft, 80°) and head straight up. Follow a rising traverse left until you are below the first ice summit, head up, and then traverse right below a rock summit and up to join a ridge. Cut below the main summit and then cut back up left and follow the ridge to the summit.

Descent: Same; 2 hours to the hut.

LA RAMPA ROUTE

Grade IV (5.5)/D (II), 75°, 600 m/2,000 ft, 5 hours

This was the normal route until the early 1990s and one of the best routes in Ecuador. Unfortunately, glacial retreat is making this route icier and harder and increasing the amount of loose rock you have to climb.

Head straight up the obvious broad couloir called La Rampa and at the top exit left. Head up the snowfields to reach the rock gullies, which are easier on the right. Climb the gullies to reach more snow and the lower summit. Drop down below the summit, traverse across rightward, and head up to join a ridge and the Normal Route.

Descent: Normal Route

SOUTH FACE ROUTE

Grade V/D+, 600 m/2,000 ft, 12 hours

OCTOBER 11–12, 1973, JOSEPH BERGÉ (FRANCE) AND MARCO CRUZ (ECUADOR)

From Laguna Amarilla southeast of Iliniza Sur, follow the south ridge and then head north. If you are unable to finish in one day, bivouac below the last ice wall. This route was originally steep ice, but it is now mainly mixed.

SOUTHEAST RIDGE ROUTE

Grade III/D, 50°, 600 m/2,000 ft, 12 hours

MARCH 24, 1974, MINARD "PETE" HALL, TRAVIS WHITE (U.S.), AND MARTIN SLATER (U.K.)

From the hut, traverse around to the base of the ridge and camp near a pond after 3 hours. (This was snow and ice in 1974, but it is now rock and scree.) Follow the ridge through mixed sections and then along the corniced ridge to the summit. The cornice can overhang on either side, and access to the summit can be barred by a mushroom cornice.

Descent: Normal Route

EAST RIDGE ROUTE (CELSO ZUQUILLO ROUTE)

Grade V/D+, 85°, 600 m/2,950 ft, 10 hours

JANUARY 1973, CELSO ZUQUILLO (ECUADOR)

Follow the east ridge to the lower summit and continue to the second, higher summit. This was originally a snow and ice route but is now mixed for at least the lower third.

SOUTHWEST FLANK ROUTE

AUGUST 21–22, 1982, JAIME MERIZALDE, OSWALDO MORALES, IVÁN VALLEJO, AND
CARLOS VÁSCONEZ (ECUADOR)

Head east for 3½ hours from the hut to reach the bottom of the route.
Head up a *canaleta* to reach the glacier. Continue straight up to a serac
wall and tunnel through it to reach a bivouac site. Traverse from east to
west to reach the summit ridge.

SOUTHWEST FACE ROUTE

Grade V/D+, 85°, 900 m/2,950 ft, 5 hours

SEPTEMBER 13, 1982, THOMAS HUNT, JORGE AND DELIA MONTOPOLI

From Loma Huinza on the Latacunga–Sigchos road, walk to the base of
the westernmost glacier (8 hours) and camp. Head up snow (40°) to get
above the first rock walls, up a steep couloir 75° for 50 m/165 ft and over
a short ice wall 85° for 5 m/16 ft to arrive 100 m/330 ft below the southwest summit ridge.

CHAPTER 8

carihuairazo

5,028 m/16,496 ft

JUNE 29, 1880, DAVID BELTRÁN, FRANCISCO JAVIER CAMPAÑA, PLUS PEDRO DE PENIPE (A
DOG) (ECUADOR), JEAN ANTOINE AND LOUIS CARREL (ITALY), AND EDWARD WHYMPER
(U.K.), WHO CLIMBED PICO MOCHA

Maps: Quero, Chimborazo

It was said that Carihuairazo was as high as its neighbor, Chimborazo, and what is now left is a remnant on the side of a 2-km/1.25-mi caldera. Edward Whymper was told "a portion of its apex fell during a great earthquake which occurred at the end of the 17th century" (*Travels*, 1892). However, there is no evidence that Carihuairazo was anywhere near as big as Chimborazo.

Carihuairazo offers Scottish-style alpine climbing, especially in the rainy season when there is more snow and the weather is surprisingly similar to Scotland in winter. However, on a good day, you get fantastic views of the north side of Chimborazo. Photos from the 1970s show a completely different mountain, one covered in snow and ice that used to be climbed via the north ridge with an easy walk up onto the summit. Because of glacial retreat, this would now be an interesting, though loose, rock route.

The word *Cari-huaira-razu* translates as either "windy snow" or "snowy/icy wind." The peak has also been known as Chimborazo-embra, or "Chimborazo's Wife."

ACCESS AND APPROACH

(See the Chimborazo and Carihuairazo map.)

From Quito's Terminal Terrestre, take a bus to Guaranda (US$3), but get off about 1¼ hours out of Ambato after the road crosses the Río Blanco. Head up the nearest hill, get a bearing on Carihuairazo, and then walk across the *páramo* to reach the base of the mountain. The walk takes 5 hours from the Ambato–Guaranda road.

Note: The rarely climbed Pico Mocha is approached from the east.

CUMBRE MÁXIMA

5,028 m/16,496 ft

MARCH 23, 1951, ARTURO EICHLER (GERMANY), JEAN MOORAWIECKI (FRANCE), AND HORACIO URIBE (COLOMBIA)

Move up the glacier, aiming for the col to the right (south) of the summit. The last 20 m/65 ft up to the ridge can be a scramble through very loose rock or an easy snow plod, depending on conditions. Follow the ridge to the summit. In snow-free conditions, there is a gap immediately before the summit, which has to be crossed to reach a 10-m/30-ft technical rock climb. In snowy conditions, it is a nice, none-too-sharp finish.

Descent: Same. A great round trip is to walk out eastward to the Panamerican Highway and then jump a bus to Quito or Riobamba. However, this takes a full day, so after climbing it is worth camping after a couple of hours of descent from high camp. When the Inca road through Abraspungo hits the valley bottom near a farm, cross the valley to the right to join the new road and follow it out to Chuquipogyo and the old cobbled Panamerican Highway. Follow this north to the old station of Urbina and then down to the new Panamerican Highway. The Inca road climbs steeply up the left side of the valley and then contours interminably before joining a vehicle track and wandering down to the old Panamerican Highway.

Ice formation on Carihuairazo with Cotopaxi in the background

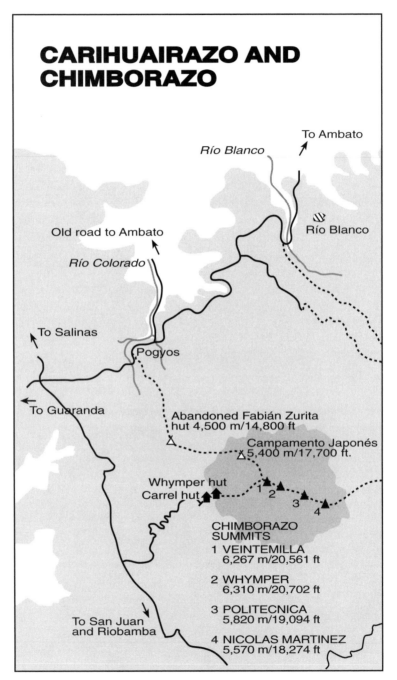

CARIHUAIRAZO AND CHIMBORAZO

To Ambato

Río Blanco

Río Blanco

Old road to Ambato

Río Colorado

To Salinas

Pogyos

To Guaranda

Abandoned Fabián Zurita hut 4,500 m/14,800 ft

Campamento Japonés 5,400 m/17,700 ft.

Whymper hut
Carrel hut

1 2
3 4

CHIMBORAZO SUMMITS

1 VEINTEMILLA
6,267 m/20,561 ft

2 WHYMPER
6,310 m/20,702 ft

3 POLITECNICA
5,820 m/19,094 ft

To San Juan and Riobamba

4 NICOLAS MARTINEZ
5,570 m/18,274 ft

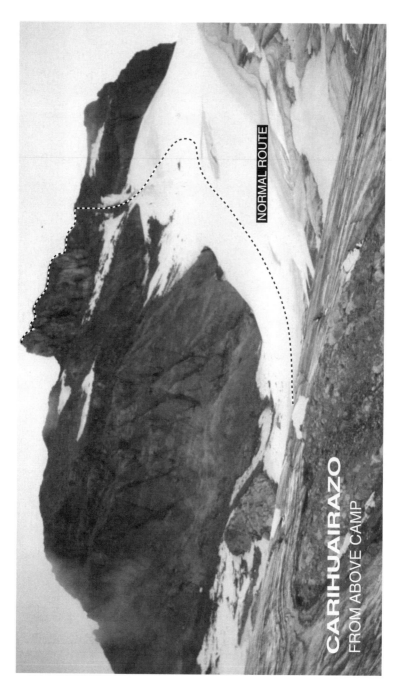

NORMAL ROUTE

CARIHUAIRAZO
FROM ABOVE CAMP

chimborazo

6,310 m/20,702 ft

JANUARY 4, 1880, JEAN ANTOINE AND LOUIS CARREL (ITALY) AND EDWARD WHYMPER (U.K.)

Maps: Chimborazo for normal routes (*Note:* The route lines and hut positions on the second-edition map are 2 km/1.25 mi too far to the east). Quero for eastern approaches, Guaranda for southern approaches.

"You, doubtless, do quite right to say that you intend to ascend

Chimborazo—a thing that everybody knows is perfectly impossible.

We know very well what is your object! You wish to discover the

TREASURES which are buried in Chimborazo."

A conversation with the Jefe Político of
Guaranda reported by Edward Whymper
Travels Amongst the Great Andes of the Equator (1892)

Chimborazo is Ecuador's highest peak, although it is not the height that impresses you but more the sheer bulk of the mountain. As Michael Koerner described the peak, it is "one of the bigger things you'll ever see" (*Fool's Climbing Guide,* 1976). To the east, Chimborazo rises 3,700 m/12,100 ft above its base, and to the west, 2,700 m/8,900 ft.

The normal routes from the southwest are one long slog—likened to "a Mont Blanc of the Andes"—however, there are interesting though high, multiday, technically difficult routes from the north, east, and south.

Chimborazo has four main summits, from the west they are as follows: Veintemilla 6,267 m/20,561 ft (named by Edward Whymper after the then president of Ecuador), Whymper 6,310 m/20,702 ft, Politécnica 5,820 m/

19,094 ft, and Nicolás Martínez
5,570 m/18,274 ft (named after
Nicolás Martínez, the "father" of
Ecuadorian mountaineering),
which although the lowest summit
is the most interesting from a climbing point of view. The Veintemilla
and Whymper summits are huge
snow domes linked by a shallow
depression that drops less than
50 m/165 ft below the summits.
The Whymper and Politécnica
summits are linked by a technically challenging ridge, while the
Nicolás Martínez summit is the
most difficult of the four and was
not climbed until 1972.

ACCESS AND APPROACH

From Quito's Terminal Terrestre,
take a bus to Riobamba (3½ hours,
US$3). In Riobamba, a taxi will
take you to the doorstep of the
lower (Carrel) hut at 4,800 m/
15,750 ft (2 hours, US$15).

Chimborazo's west face

Jeep hire from Quito takes 4½ hours and is US$140 for up to four
people, US$35 for each additional person up to nine.

From the Carrel hut it is a 30-minute slow walk to the higher
(Whymper) refuge at 5,000 m/16,400 ft. Both refuges are guarded, have
gas and water, and cost US$10 per person per night.

CUMBRE WHYMPER (MÁXIMA, ECUADOR)

6,310 m/20,702 ft

JANUARY 4, 1880, JEAN ANTOINE AND LOUIS CARREL (ITALY) AND EDWARD WHYMPER (U.K.)

The choice of which normal route to climb—El Castillo or the Original Whymper Route—depends on the prevalent conditions. Given the
choice, the El Castillo Route is objectively safer. However, in the late
1990s, neither route was safely possible in its entirety. The safest way up

was to start with the Thielmann Glacier Direct Route and then traverse left to the El Castillo Route, joining it above El Castillo. Whichever route you choose, an early start is essential before the sun turns the snow to sugar and increases the avalanche risk.

EL CASTILLO ROUTE

Grade II/PD, 40°, 1,300 m/4,250 ft, 7–9 hours

From the hut, follow the path up the left side of the stream, heading straight for the large rock outcrop on the skyline called El Castillo. Cross the stream and zigzag up, following paths through scree to reach a shallow basin below the left end of the obvious terrace—El Corredor—below El Castillo. Move up to the terrace, gain it by often a short steep couple of moves (70°, 3 m/10 ft), and then traverse rightward along it to reach broader and crevassed ice fields. Zigzag up to reach the northwest ridge above and to the right of El Castillo. Follow the ridge to the Veintemilla and then Whymper summits.

Descent: Same; 2 to 4 hours.

THIELMANN GLACIER DIRECT ROUTE

Grade III/AD+, 60°, 1,300 m/4,250 ft, 8 hours

From the Whymper hut, head straight up to the tongue of the Thielmann Glacier (normally the lowest part of glacier visible from the hut). Join the glacier (hard ice-gravel in dry conditions) and work a route up through the crevasses until you are below the Veintemilla summit. Head left to avoid being below the rock bands and seracs and then head up right to the Veintemilla summit and continue to the Whymper summit.

Descent: El Castillo Route (2 to 4 hours)

WEST FACE ROUTE

Grade V/TD, 85°, 1,300 m/4,250 ft, 9–10 hours

1996, STEVE HOUSE (U.S.) SOLO

This route is only occasionally in condition. Staying to the right of the Thielmann Glacier, climb ice runnels and mixed sections up to the Original Whymper Route. Instead of following the Original Whymper Route left, continue straight up to the Whymper summit, going through the seracs.

Descent: El Castillo or Original Whymper Routes

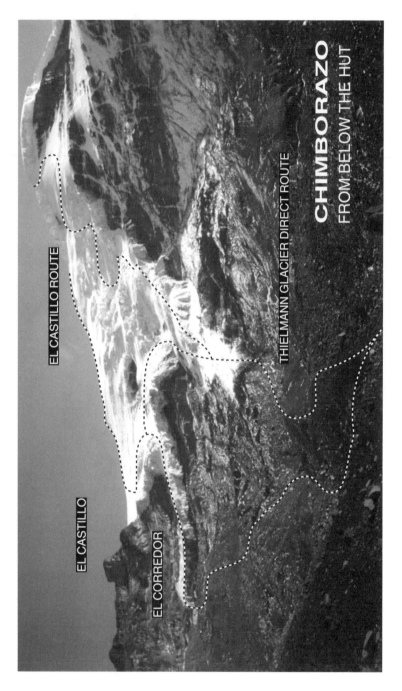

CHIMBORAZO
FROM BELOW THE HUT

THIELMANN GLACIER DIRECT ROUTE

EL CASTILLO ROUTE

EL CASTILLO

EL CORREDOR

ORIGINAL WHYMPER ROUTE (SOUTHWEST RIDGE)

Grade II/PD, 40°, 1,300 m/4,250 ft, 9 hours

From the hut, go up scree to join the southwest ridge that heads up toward the right of the visible Veintemilla summit. Continue up until you are below the Southern Walls. Traverse left under the large serac wall and cut back up right to join the El Castillo Route to the Veintemilla summit. Continue on to the Whymper summit.

Note: Unless a major amount of good snow and ice is on the mountain to hold together the loose rock, this route is threatened by rockfall and serac collapse.

Descent: Same; 2 to 4 hours.

DIRECTÍSIMA FROM THE SOUTHEAST VIA THE TOTORILLAS GLACIER

JULY 23–24, 1939, GOTTFRIED HIRTZ, WILFRID KÜHM (GERMANY), ISIDORO FORMAGGIO, AND PIERO GHIGLIONE (ITALY). ALSO A VARIANT TO THE RIGHT FINISHING UP A 75° SERAC, 1987, ALBERTO CAMPANILE (ITALY)

This route is an aesthetically pleasing one. From Whymper's Chamonix Aiguilles on the southwest ridge, go to the right, cross the Glaciar de Escombros (Debris Glacier), and head direct to the Whymper summit.

Note: There can be major rockfall danger from the Southern Walls.

Descent: Original Whymper or El Castillo Routes

MURALLAS ROJAS ROUTE

Grade II/PD, 45°, 1,000 m/3,300 ft, 8 hours from high camp

JULY 3, 1880, DAVID BELTRÁN, FRANCISCO JAVIER CAMPAÑA (ECUADOR), JEAN ANTOINE AND LOUIS CARREL (ITALY), AND EDWARD WHYMPER (U.K.)

This was the normal route up Chimborazo until the opening of the Whymper hut in 1980 encouraged climbers to attempt the mountain from the other side. Thierry Renard (France) descended the route on skis in 1979.

Access and Approach

From Pogyos on the Ambato–Guaranda Road to the northwest of the mountain, cross the volcanic arenal to reach the site of the Fabián Zurita hut (opened in 1964), also known as the Nido de Condores at 4,500 m/ 14,800 ft.

Head up toward the northwest ridge to beneath the Murallas Rojas (Red or Northern Walls), staying to the right to reach Campamento Japonés at 5,400 m/17,700 ft.

From camp, move up toward the Murallas Rojas (Red Walls) at about 5,700 m/18,700 ft and then turn right (west) to go around the right end of the rock wall before cutting back left. This is the steepest section of the route. (*Note:* It is also possible to go to the left or east of the Murallas Rojas.) Zigzag up to join the Original Whymper Route, but stay to the left and below the Veintemilla summit and continue directly to the Whymper summit.

Descent: Same or El Castillo Route.

CUMBRE POLITÉCNICA (CENTRAL)

5,820 m/19,094 ft

MAY 30, 1971, ADOLFO HOLGUÍN, LEONARDO MENESES, CÉSAR ORTÍZ, SANTIAGO RIVADENEIRA, RAMIRO SÁENZ, AND DIEGO TERÁN (ECUADOR) VIA THE BOUSSINGAULT GLACIER

From the Tortorillas valley to the southeast of the mountain, gain the Boussingault Glacier and head for the col between the Politécnica and Whymper summits. From the col, turn right to reach the summit. The climb takes 8 hours up, 4 hours down.

CUMBRE NICOLÁS MARTÍNEZ

5,570 m/18,274 ft

SEPTEMBER 14, 1972, JERZY DOBRZYSKY, GUSTAV GRIZEZ, AND ANDRZY PAULO (POLAND) VIA THE GARCÍA MORENO GLACIER

Cumbre Nicolás Martínez is the lowest but technically most interesting of Chimborazo's main peaks. A number of routes have been done, but detailed descriptions are hard to find.

ARISTA DEL SOL (NORTHEAST RIDGE)

Grade V (5.7)/TD (V), 85°, 900 m/3,000 ft, 10 hours

JULY 3, 1983, JORGE ANHALZER, R. CÁRDENAS, AND RAMIRO NAVERETTE (ECUADOR)

Access and Approach

Via the old Urbina railway station just off the Panamerican Highway, it is possible to drive to 4,300 m/14,100 ft and then hike upward through *páramo* to reach possible camping at 4,700 m/15,400 ft after 3 hours. Allegedly, this route is one of the best in Ecuador. Follow the rock ridge that separates the García Moreno and Teodoro Wolf Glaciers. The first two-thirds of the route is mainly rock and mixed ground before you join the glacier and continue up on snow and ice.

Descent: Same; or continue up and traverse the mountain, descending to the hut.

TRAVERSES (INTEGRAL)

FIRST TRAVERSE: DECEMBER 19, 1979, FREDY KÄLIN AND RES MENZI (SWITZERLAND) VIA THE BOUSSINGAULT GLACIER TO THE SHOULDER BETWEEN THE POLITÉCNICA AND WHYMPER SUMMITS, FOLLOWING THE EAST RIDGE TO THE MAIN SUMMIT AND DESCENDING VIA THE NORMAL ROUTE

All traverses are long and require at least one camp at about 6,000 m/ 19,700 ft. Difficulties recede once you reach the Nicolás Martínez summit, but moving from the Politécnica to Whymper summits is hard going. After that, you are normally just left with deep, soft snow until you start the descent. Retreat is difficult.

Starting at the García Moreno Glacier to the southeast of the mountain and bivouac, climb the Nicolás Martínez and then Politécnica peaks before establishing a second bivouac. Continue the next day over the Whymper and Veintemilla summits before you descend via one of the normal routes.

The Integral has also been done starting with the Arista del Sol (December 27–30, 1989).

Chimborazo's northeast side from the Llanganates

CHAPTER 10

imbabura

4,630 m/15,190 ft

FIRST ASCENT PROBABLY PRE-HISPANIC; FIRST RECORDED ASCENT SEPTEMBER 14, 1802,

FRANCISCO JOSÉ DE CALDAS (COLOMBIA) AND SALVADOR CHUQUÍN (ECUADOR)

Map: San Pablo del Lago

A large hill with a long walk up it, Imbabura is good for acclimatization and fitness. It was glaciated and people used to bring down ice to what is now the handicrafts center of Otavalo. The mountain stands above Lago San Pablo, close to Otavalo, but the most convenient route starts on the other side of the mountain. Climbing from this side also gives you the best views of the impressive open caldera.

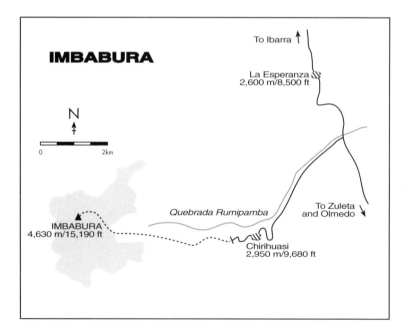

ACCESS

Either take a bus directly to Ibarra from Quito's Terminal Terrestre (2½ hours, US$2.50) or take a bus to Otavalo (2 hours, US$2) and then take a local bus on to Ibarra. In Ibarra, take a bus to La Esperanza (30 minutes, US$0.20).

It is best to go in the day before and spend the night in La Esperanza. There are three basic places to stay in La Esperanza, the best being Casa Aída.

Jeep hire from Quito is US$80 for up to four people, US$20 for each additional person up to nine. If you do hire a jeep, go out via Zuleta, Olmedo, and Cayambe for a look at some traditional highland Ecuadorian countryside.

APPROACH

La Esperanza is situated at 2,600 m/8,500 ft, which leaves 2,000 m/6,600 ft of vertical ascent if you start in the village. Rather usefully, on most days buses pass through La Esperanza at 5:30 A.M., traveling the 4 km/2.5 mi to the village of Chirihuasi 2,950 m/9,680 ft. This saves 1½ hours of walking. In dry conditions, a four-wheel-drive vehicle could get to 3,200 m/10,500 ft, but don't rely on it.

NORMAL ROUTE

Note: There is no water on this route above the village of Chirihuasi.

From La Esperanza, continue along the road heading away from Ibarra and turn right immediately before the bridge over the Quebrada Rumipamba. Continue up the cobbled road, through Chirihuasi and up the new dirt road. The road zigzags, but the path heads straight up staying on the left (south) side of the Quebrada Rumipamba valley. The road becomes a track at about 3,200 m/10,500 ft.

Follow the track up along the ridge. The track becomes a path and then hooks around to the right before continuing up to a water tank at about 3,450 m/11,320 ft.

From the water tank, either push through the vegetation and follow the old path straight up the ridge or follow the good path off to the right and then cut back left to the ridge from where the path is good again and stays with the ridge.

Imbabura and Lago San Pablo

After 1 hour the path leaves the ridge at about 4,085 m/13,400 ft and heads off left before climbing back up right to the ridge 25 minutes later, joining it at about 4,200 m/13,780 ft.

Continue along the ridge path to the summit in another hour, dropping down shortly twice before climbing again. There is a 2 m/6 ft scramble up onto the summit block.

Descent: Same

cayambe

5,789 m/18,993 ft

APRIL 4, 1880, JEAN ANTOINE AND LOUIS CARREL (ITALY) AND EDWARD WHYMPER (U.K.)

Maps: Cayambe (although the road to the hut is not marked), Nevado Cayambe

This peak is the highest and coldest point on the equator. It is the only place on earth where the latitude is 0° and so is the temperature. Unfortunately, zero visibility is also common because of Cayambe's eastern location, although the mountain is often visible from Quito. As a result, it is highly recommended to flag the route on the way up, so you can find your way back across some very large and relatively featureless glaciers.

The name comes from the Caranqui word *kayan,* meaning "ice," or the Quichua *cahan* or *caxan,* meaning "very cold high place." Another interpretation is from Quitu and translates as "water, the source of life."

Long thought extinct, Cayambe is now deemed to be an active volcano, and it is constantly monitored. It is common to smell sulfur while climbing, although the vent high on the mountain is yet to be found. Edward Whymper climbed from the rocky outcrop of Punta Jarrin, crossing the top of the Espinosa Glacier—the two features named by Whymper after the then-owner of the mountain and the Hacienda Guachalá, Antonio Jarrin de Espinosa. However, he did not approach from the north, as is often stated, but took about the most direct line from Cayambe to Punta Jarrin following the valley of the Río Monjas. Since the hut was opened in March 1979, very few people go in from any other direction, but the route from the north is far more attractive. It gives better views of the mountain, the routefinding is easier, and you have a higher chance of seeing condors during the approach from the north.

Whichever route you choose, it is worth checking out the route to the glacier the day before climbing to avoid losing time wandering around in the dark. It is essential to flag the route on the glacier because clouds normally roll in from the jungle during the morning, reducing visibility to not a lot. An early start is essential owing to the high avalanche risk once

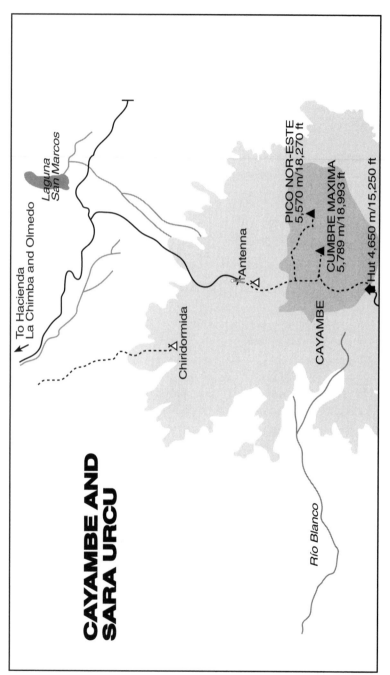

CAYAMBE AND SARA URCU

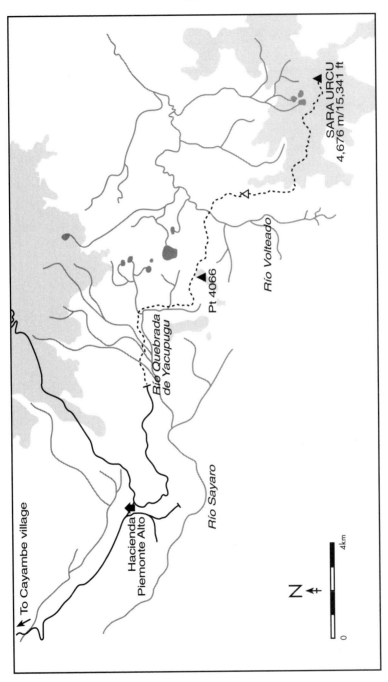

SARA URCU
4,676 m/15,341 ft

Río Volteado

Pt 4066

Río Quebrada
de Yacupugu

Río Sayaro

To Cayambe village

Hacienda
Piemonte Alto

N

0   4km

the sun begins to melt the snow. The pioneer of the current Normal Route, Frenchman Joseph Bergé, together with Ecuadorians Carlos Oleas and César Ruales were killed in an avalanche on Cayambe in April 1974.

Note: The walk out from Cayambe is very long, whichever way you go. If you follow the road it will take forever, much of it is made of foot-breaking cobbles, and outside of weekends you are unlikely to see any vehicles. Allegedly, a milk truck comes from Hacienda Piemonte Alto. The Hacienda can be reached in about 4 hours from the hut, and you could ask permission to camp the night before getting a lift in the truck. The shortest walk out follows the Río Blanco valley and can get you to Cayambe village in about 6 hours from the hut. It is far more comfortable to arrange for a jeep or pickup.

ACCESS

For all routes it is necessary to go through the village of Cayambe. A bus from Quito's Terminal Terrestre to the village takes 1½ hours and costs US$1.15.

ACCESS FOR THE NORMAL ROUTE

Arrange transport from the main square in Cayambe for the 1¾-hour journey to the hut at 4,650 m/15,250 ft. A four-wheel-drive vehicle can make it to the front door of the hut, but a pickup will make it only to the zigzags, 1½ hours from the village, US$18, leaving a 30- to 60-minute walk to the hut. (A milk truck leaves around 6:00 A.M. from outside the

Reaching the col with Cumbre Norte in the background, Cayambe Normal Route

hospital in Cayambe and goes to Hacienda Piemonte Alto for US$0.50, but you will then have to walk to the hut—4 hours or more uphill.)

The road goes past a Reserva Cayambe–Coca office at Piemonte Alto (marked Pitana on the IGM map) where, if it is open, you will be charged US$10 to enter the reserve. Immediately after the reserve office there is a T-junction. Turn left to get to the hut. The hut has fantastic views of Glaciar Hermosa, bunks, running water, gas stoves, and a few pans and costs US$10 per person, per night. It is staffed and there is a radio.

Jeep hire from Quito is US$100 for up to four people US$20 for each additional person up to nine.

ACCESS FROM THE NORTH

The traditional way to climb Cayambe before the hut was built was from Hacienda La Chimba in Olmedo, north of the mountain, using mules for the 6-hour walk in to Chiridormida and then going for the summit in one long day or making another high camp before the summit push. It is faster and requires less effort to drive farther, either hiring a jeep from one of the Quito agencies with a driver who knows where he is going or using public transport.

From Cayambe village, hire a pickup traveling via Olmedo and then continue on in the direction of Laguna San Marcos. There is a sometimes-staffed Reserva Cayambe–Coca Inefan station to pass through where, if open, you will be charged US$10 to enter the reserve. About 40 minutes after passing Hacienda La Chimba, a good turn off to the right leads up to staffed police and army antenna stations in another 20 minutes. A four-wheel-drive vehicle can get 300 m/1,000 ft farther following a track over the grass. Jeep hire from Quito is US$140 for up to four people, US$35 for each additional person up to nine.

CUMBRE MÁXIMA

5,789 m/18,993 ft

APRIL 4, 1880, JEAN ANTOINE AND LOUIS CARREL (ITALY) AND EDWARD WHYMPER (U.K.)

NORMAL ROUTE

Grade II/PD, 35°, 1,200 m/3,900 ft, 7 hours

From the hut, head up and over the rock ridge above the hut, drop down, and head up to join the glacier. Once on the glacier, head left

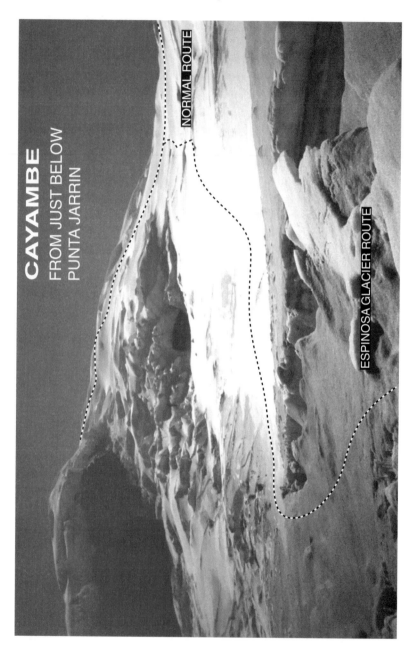

CAYAMBE
FROM JUST BELOW
PUNTA JARRIN

NORMAL ROUTE

ESPINOSA GLACIER ROUTE

toward Punta Jarrin, staying to the right of the rocky outcrop.

From above Punta Jarrin, head up left toward the summit, working a way through the multitude of crevasses, many of which can be stepped over but a considerable number must be gone around. The crux of the route is getting over, around, or through the large crevasse that is normally open about 200 m/650 ft below the summit. This can involve climbing down into the crevasse and out on the other side or traversing along its edge until an easy crossing is found. After passing the large crevasse, head up to the col to the right of the north summit (the one with a rock band underneath it), turn right, and continue along to the main summit.

The subsidiary peaks of Cumbre Norte 5,739 m/18,828 ft (left/north of the main summit) and Cumbre Oriental 5,715 m/18,749 ft (east of the main summit) were climbed July 21–24, 1964, by Kazutaka Aoki, Keinosuke Matsumura, Susumu Murata, and Ichiro Yoshizawa (Japan). They can both be climbed within 30 minutes from the main summit, either on the way up or down.

Descent: Same

ESPINOSA GLACIER ROUTE

Grade II/PD, 50°, 1,000 m/3,300 ft, 5 hours

Approaching from the north, follow the ridge leading from the antenna south toward the col between Punta Jarrin and the main summit. The path contours right into a broad, flat-bottomed valley (45 minutes). Cross the sediment-filled stream to the left and then follow the grassed moraine ridge that becomes a rock moraine shortly before its high point (1 hour). Follow the ridge to its end (30 minutes) and then drop down right to the glacier. There are some flat spots for a camp on the rock outcrop in the center of the glacier at 4,900 m/16,075 ft with clear run-off water. Finding a way there is tricky because of the number of crevasses (2 hours).

Move to the right side of the glacier above the rock outcrop and carry on up to reach the broad col between Punta Jarrin and the summit (2 hours). Join the Normal Route and follow it as above.

Descent: Same; 1 hour to the col, 1 hour to the rock outcrop, 1 hour to the bottom of the glacier.

PICO NOR-ESTE

ESPINOSA GLACIER ROUTE

NORMAL ROUTE

CAYAMBE
FROM NEAR THE ANTENNA TO THE NORTH

PICO NOR-ESTE

5,570 m/18,270 ft

NORMAL ROUTE

Grade III-/AD, 60°, 700 m/2,300 ft, 3 hours from the glacier

FEBRUARY OR MARCH 1976, LUIS CAMACHO, JACINTO CARRASCO, AND PATRICIO RAMÓN

(ECUADOR)

This beautiful and rarely climbed peak gives fantastic views of the east side of Cayambe.

The approach is the same as for the Espinosa Glacier Route above. It is possible to climb the route from camp near the antenna station. To shorten the climb, put in a camp somewhere between the end of the track and the glacier, which is 4 hours from the road's beginning.

From the antenna station, follow the ridge south until it drops down to the grassy and boggy plain. Cross the plain and head up on the other side. Follow another ridge up and then traverse. Avoid going higher than 4,800 m/15,750 ft because you will arrive at a cliff section and have to descend, but stay higher than 4,600 m/15,100 ft or you will cross the valley and then be faced by a cliff section.

Drop down to the glacier coming down from Cayambe's main peak, cross it, and then head up a broad but narrowing snow gully to reach the glacier that comes down from the col between the northeast peak (on the left) and the main summit massif (on the right). Head up the glacier, working a way through the innumerable crevasses to reach the col. Turn left and continue to the summit.

Descent: Same

OTHER ROUTES

FROM THE NORTH, AUGUST 9, 1988, ERIC LAWRIE, PHIL TOWNSEND (U.K.), AND DAVID

PURDY (U.S.)

From Laguna San Marcos, head up to the glacier at the base of the north face. Climb the north face and then the north buttress to a bivouac 100 m/300 ft below the summit.

Descent: Normal Route

sara urcu

4,676 m/15,341 ft

APRIL 17, 1880, JEAN ANTOINE AND LOUIS CARREL (ITALY) AND EDWARD WHYMPER (U.K.)

Maps: Cangahua, Cerro Sara Urcu, plus Cayambe to cover the entire approach

Sara Urcu offers a true wilderness experience and is probably the least-climbed of Ecuador's peaks—the second ascent was not until 1955, 75 years after Edward Whymper spent 17 days finding and climbing the peak. Some of Whymper's comments are worth remembering before planning to climb this mountain: "the whole country was a dismal swamp; and everlasting rain was falling . . . had to stop in a swamp, on a spot where, if you stood still, you sank up to the knees in slime . . . having to pass through country more difficult than any we had hitherto traversed. . . . The whole country was like a saturated sponge" (*Travels,* 1892).

The summit ridge of Sara Urcu

Sara Urcu has Ecuador's easternmost glacier, and it is one of the country's lowest. After days of wandering through bogs and dense vegetation, you will need crampons and an ice ax to climb.

If lucky, you might see deer, spectacled bears, and tapir, as well as views of the south side of Cayambe, the east of Antisana, and Cotopaxi. Unfortunately, the area suffers from very poor visibility, so it is also possible to spend 4 days here and not see anything. This is the kind of place you wish manufacturers of allegedly waterproof clothing and footwear would come to before marketing their products. You will get wet either from the rain; from walking through marshes, bogs, and streams; or from pushing through chest-high wet vegetation or, most likely, a combination of all these. On top of this, the dense vegetation and lack of paths make the ground as dangerous as any glacier—repeated falls into concealed holes have a high leg-breaking potential.

Note: Maps, a compass, and the ability to use them are essential—people have gotten very, very lost getting in and out of Sara Urcu. To mount a search in the area would be practically impossible because of the terrain, the vegetation, and the standard poor visibility. Paths before the Río Volteado tend to be made by cows, paths beyond the river by deer and bears. They can be helpful for short periods, but keep your map and compass out.

Sara Urcu can be climbed in 4 days:

Day 1: Go from Quito to Cayambe village and to the end of the road by vehicle and then hike to and cross the Río Volteado.

Day 2: Continue up and place a high camp in an easily identifiable spot because of the likelihood of returning in poor visibility.

Day 3: Summit and begin the walk out.

Day 4: Head back to the end of the road and take transport back to Cayambe village and Quito.

ACCESS

(See the Cayambe and Sara Urcu map.)

Follow the access and approach directions for Cayambe to Cayambe village and then continue on to Hacienda Piemonte Alto (marked Pitana on the IGM map) where there is a Reserva Cayambe–Coca office where you must pay US$10 for entry, if it is open. Beyond the office is a T-junction; turn right and the cobblestones soon finish. Continue along the road for 8 km/5 mi until you reach the point where it was cut by a landslide.

APPROACH

Day 1: Cross the landslide and follow the road up for 100 m/330 ft until you see a broad green area heading off to the right. Follow this, cross the living polylepis tree bridge, and follow the paths to what looks like a bus shelter but is in fact a covered cattle trough. From the trough,

SOUTHWEST RIDGE ROUTE

SARA URCU
FROM IMMEDIATELY
BEFORE JOINING THE
GLACIER

follow the paths up-valley and then across the marsh, aiming to arrive at the edge still to the north of the Río Quebrada de Yacupugu.

Contour around, staying to the east of the river, and enter its valley, staying above the marsh and below the low cliffs. When the cliffs end, head up and left into another marsh area. Move to the right (south) of the marsh and head to a point immediately north of Point 4066 on the IGM map. From here, drop to the Río Volteado, which is recognizable by its series of S-shaped meanders (5 hours).

Cross the Volteado opposite the two waterfalls and then head up the left side of either waterfall. (The path up the side of the lower [northern] waterfall is clearer.) When the slope slackens off, start going right and looking for a dryish spot to camp (2 hours).

Day 2: Keep heading south, but resist the temptation to go up to the ridge—it is farther than it looks, and you cannot follow the ridge around—because parts are too steep. Keep the ridge on your left as you drop into, cross, and then rise up out of a series of boggy flat bits. Cross a broad marsh area and then reach a valley, which drops steeply to the right and rises to the left. Go up and left, cross the stream to reach the right side of the valley, and head up to a rocky ridge. Aim for the right end of the rocky ridge, cross it, and follow the clear path that traverses below the ridge on the other side. When you reach the end of the traverse, drop to the col, cross it, and make a way through the rocky ground, staying above the rock slabs to arrive above the glacier. To reach the glacier, either scramble along the left side of the glacier through large fallen blocks or drop to the small terminal moraine lake (5 hours).

SOUTHWEST RIDGE ROUTE

Grade II (5.3)/PD (II), 40°, 250 m/800 ft, 45 minutes from the start of the glacier

Head up the left side of the glacier. The glacier is disappearing—it is amazing that it has lasted so long—and it can be cut by emerging rock. Continue up to the ridge and turn right. Follow the ridge and stay to the left of the first rock peak to reach the second and third peaks, which are the highest—the second peak is marked by a small cairn.

Descent: Same

antisana (antizana)

5,758 m/18,891 ft

MARCH 10, 1880, JEAN ANTOINE AND LOUIS CARREL (ITALY) AND EDWARD WHYMPER (U.K.)

Maps: Papallacta, Laguna de Mica. (If you are coming from the south, use Pintag and Sincholagua if you want every step of the way covered.)

Big, high, and covered in crevasses, Antisana is pretty wild and has some of the most interesting climbing in Ecuador. The base of the volcano measures 14 km/8.75 mi north to south. The mountain was a huge caldera 1,800 m/5,900 ft across and 1,000 m/3,300 ft deep, but only the west side is left after a massive prehistoric explosion. The volcano is, however, listed as active and is monitored. According to some, the name has no translation; others say it is from the Quichua *anti* (high place) and *sani* (dark abode). On the approaches to the mountain, keep your eyes open for condors, kestrels, and other birds. When camped, keep your food wrapped to protect it from *páramo* wolves (a type of fox) that will scavenge around camps. Deer are also sometimes seen.

Despite Ecuadorian law stating that no land over 4,000 m/13,100 ft can be owned, you have to cross land owned by the Hacienda Antisana to reach the mountain and for this you need written permission. You have to show your permit at a first checkpoint, and it will then be collected at a second checkpoint. Permits cost US$10 per person and are available from the hacienda owner José Delgado in Quito (telephone 435828, fax 462013). To get your permit, you need to go to his house in Calle Sarmiento de Gamboa next to number 552.

ACCESS

Option 1: Hire a jeep from one of the Quito agencies that knows the route and how to get the permission. This will get you to within 20 minutes of camp at the base of the glacier in less than 3 hours for US$150 (return double).

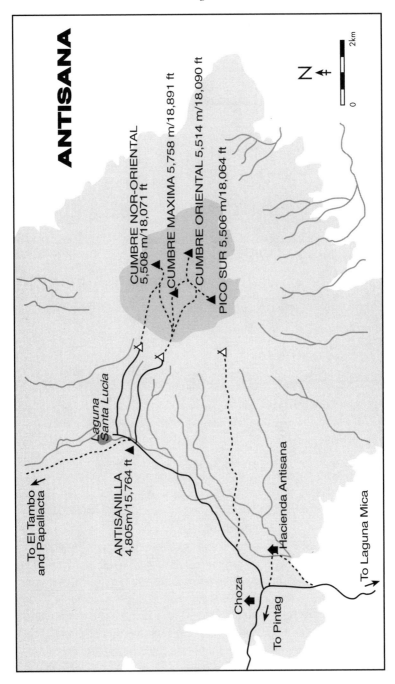

ANTISANA

CUMBRE NOR-ORIENTAL
5,508 m/18,071 ft

CUMBRE MAXIMA 5,758 m/18,891 ft

CUMBRE ORIENTAL 5,514 m/18,090 ft

PICO SUR 5,506 m/18,064 ft

Laguna
Santa Lucia

ANTISANILLA
4,805m/15,764 ft

To El Tambo
and Papallacta

Hacienda Antisana

To Laguna Mica

Choza

To Pintag

N

0   2km

Cumbre Oriental Antisana

Note: All water at the camp is heavily sedimented. Bring all the water you will need by jeep, and camp at the end of the track to avoid having to carry it up to camp. Alternatively, reach camp and then continue to the glacier where there is clear runoff during the day.

Option 2: Take a bus from below Plaza La Marin near Quito's Terminal Terrestre to Pintag (1 hour, US$0.50). In Pintag hire a pickup to Laguna Santa Lucia (2 hours, US$40). Follow the new asphalt road to the first gate and show your permit. Continue along the good road to a barrier where you hand in your permit and continue to the thatched *choza* of Santa Lucia, a farm with allegedly 10,000 sheep (it smells like it on some days).

At the Santa Lucia *choza,* turn left and follow the road to the point where it drops down to a stream before rising up on the other side to a place where construction material—like that used for the road you are on—is being ripped out of a lava flow. At this point make a switchback turn left off the road and follow a faint track that joins up with a more distinct track heading north after 100 m/109 yd. Follow this track until you are due east (right) of the highest (middle) of Antisanilla's three peaks. It would be unwise to take any non-four-wheel-drive vehicle farther.

From here head east, crossing the stream (last clear water) and following the often-faint vehicle track toward Antisana (2 hours).

A great round trip—especially in dry conditions—is to go in via Pintag, climb, and then walk out to the Quito road west of Papallacta and flag down a bus: go up and left to get back to Quito or down and right for the hot springs in Papallacta (which means "country of potatoes" according to some). The walk out from Laguna Santa Lucia takes 3 hours to Laguna Volcán and another 3 hours to the road at kilometer 41 in El Tambo. From here the bus takes 1¾ hours to Quito and costs US$1.40.

CUMBRE MÁXIMA

5,758 m/18,891 ft

MARCH 10, 1880, JEAN ANTOINE AND LOUIS CARREL (ITALY) AND EDWARD WHYMPER (U.K.)

NORMAL ROUTE

Grade II+/AD-, 40°,1,000 m/3,300 ft, 6 hours

From camp below the sediment-filled glacial ponds, follow the path right (south) to the moraine ridge. Follow the ridge to the end and drop down right to the glacier (1 hour).

Head southeast toward the col between the main and south summits, following a rising traverse and avoiding the crevasses. There can be a serac section to work through before heading up toward the summit.

A steeper variation of the Normal Route involves heading up to the left of the smaller left-hand of the two rock outcrops and then working a way up to the right (southern) end of the summit plateau.

The Normal Route goes to the right of the larger (right-hand) rock outcrop, up toward the ridge linking the main and south summits. Turn left and follow it to arrive at the right (southern) end of the summit plateau.

The summit is normally surrounded on the north, west, and south sides by a large crevasse. If there are no obvious bridges, it can sometimes be possible to drop down into the crevasse, step across it when it is sufficiently narrow, and then climb steeply out (up to 90°). Another possibility is to go up to the ridge linking the main and south summits and look for a longer but easier way around by heading east and then moving gently up on to the summit plateau.

Descent: Same; 2 hours to the end of the glacier, 30 minutes up and down the moraine ridge to camp.

WEST FACE DIRECT ROUTE

Grade II+/AD-, 65°,1,000 m/3,300 ft, 6 hours

MINARD "PETE" HALL, STAN HUNCILMAN (U.S.), TONY BURKE, ALLAN MILLER, MARTIN AND

SHIRLEY SLATER (U.K.), JAIME DELGADO, JAVIER SILVA, AND THELMO AND DIGNA

VALLADORES (ECUADOR)

This is the best route up to the highest peak. It is more direct—and therefore steeper—than the Normal Route, but routefinding is much easier as is crossing the crevasse below the summit to reach the summit plateau.

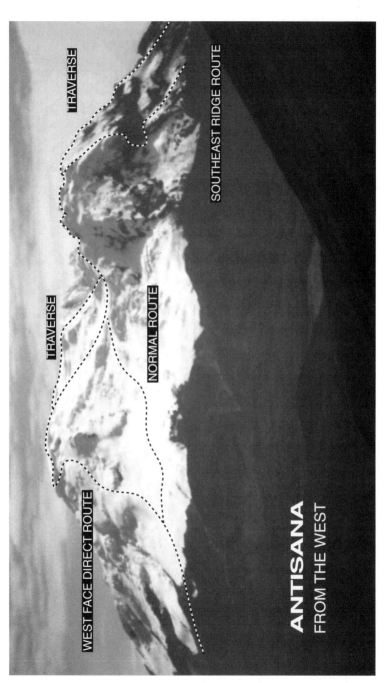

TRAVERSE

SOUTHEAST RIDGE ROUTE

TRAVERSE

NORMAL ROUTE

WEST FACE DIRECT ROUTE

ANTISANA
FROM THE WEST

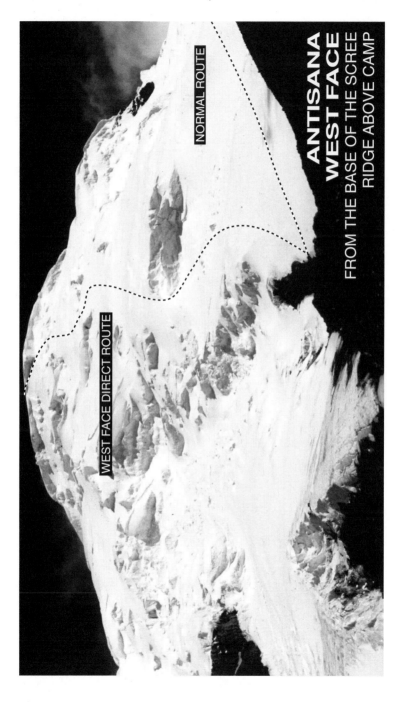

Glacier camp on Antisana's west face

The approach and start to the route are the same as for the Normal Route. From the glacier, head straight up aiming for the prominent snow/ice formation in the summit crevasse that looks like the prow of a ship—this is easily visible as one side is normally in shadow and the other in sunlight. It is necessary to cross and turn a number of crevasses, but the line is clear. The bergschrund opened wider in 1999, making the final 80 m/260 ft impassible. It might be possible to go farther north.

From the prow, head left (north) along a narrow snow ridge that rises to the top of the summit crevasse. Cross the crevasse and keep going up-hill to reach the summit.

Descent: Same; 3 hours.

CUMBRE NOR-ORIENTAL (PICO NOR-ESTE, NORTHEAST SUMMIT)

5,508 m/18,071 ft

Grade IV/D+, 80°, 900 m/2,950 ft from camp, 8 hours

DECEMBER 30, 1972, LEONARDO MENESES, SANTIAGO RIVANDENEIRA, AND HUGO TORRES (ECUADOR)

The Cumbre Nor-Oriental is staggeringly beautiful when seen from the main summit of Antisana, resembling a fairytale picture of a mountain.

**ANTISANA
CUMBRE NOR-ORIENTAL**
FROM BELOW THE MAIN SUMMIT

NORTHEAST RIDGE ROUTE

From the north it is much less impressive and looks like some minor ridge.

The route proper starts from a col between the main and northeast peaks. There are two ways to reach the start of the route, and neither of them involves going over the main summit—steep ice cliffs and large crevasses prevent this access. Either use the same camp as for the Normal Route, head straight up onto the glacier, and then head diagonally left to the col or, instead of turning right at Antisanilla on the way in, continue up until just before Laguna Santa Lucia, turn right, and follow the track toward Antisana. Before you reach the meteorological measuring equipment, turn right and continue up the faint track to a group of waterless flat grassy spots 10 m/yd from the start of the moraine. Cross the moraine and move up the glacier to the col.

After you reach the col, there is relatively little vertical height left to climb, but the route becomes increasingly technical. At the col, turn left (northeast) and follow the ridge to the summit over snow and ice up to 80°. The ridge is heavily corniced to the right (south).

Descent: Same

CUMBRE ORIENTAL (PICO ESTE, EAST SUMMIT)

5,514 m/18,090 ft

Grade IV+/TD-, 85°, 200 m/660 ft, 6 hours

FEBRUARY 26, 1974, MIGUEL ANDRADE AND HUGO TORRES (ECUADOR)

Slightly less impressive than its northern neighbor, the Cumbre Oriental is a harder and more exposed climb. For this reason, it makes sense to put in a high camp near the col between the main and south summits. To reach this point, either follow the Normal Route up or climb the West Face Direct Route and then go over the summit plateau and down on the other side.

From the col, follow the east ridge out. Rappel down 60 m/200 ft to the cleft in the ridge, leaving a rope in place to speed up the return, and then climb steeply up to the summit staying on the ridge.

Descent: Same; rappel back down to the cleft and then prussik or jumar up the other side.

EAST RIDGE ROUTE

ANTISANA
CUMBRE ORIENTAL
FROM BELOW THE MAIN SUMMIT

PICO SUR (CUMBRE SUR-ORIENTAL)

5,506 m/18,064 ft

NOVEMBER 1963, ANDREW GRUFT (SOUTH AFRICA) AND DICK JONES (U.S.). DISPUTED BY ECUADORIANS WHO CLAIM THE FIRST ASCENT FOR AUGUST 22, 1964, EDDIE BERNBAUM (U.S.), LEONARDO DROIRA, AND RÓMULO PAMIÑO (ECUADOR).

Climbing the Pico Sur, the hardest of Antisana's four peaks, can involve hard rock climbing and/or steep snow and ice at high altitude. Pico Sur is sometimes inaccurately called Antisanilla, which is in fact the small rock peak to the west of Antisana.

Approach

The approach is the same as for the Normal Route above, but after Santa Lucia, head north, keeping a lookout for a track leading east toward the Pico Sur. A jeep can get some of the way in. Set up camp as close to the glacier as possible for clear water or, better, take extra fuel and set up a camp below the col between the main and south peaks.

FIGURE S ROUTE

Grade IV-/D, 65°, 650 m/2,100 ft, 6 hours from high camp beneath the col

NOVEMBER 3, 1982, JORGE ANHALZER, FABIÁN CÁCERES, DANNY MORENO, MAURICIO REINOSO, NELSON DE LA TORRE, AND HUGO TORRES (ECUADOR)

Go around to the right of the peak to avoid the lowest rock section. Cut back left and follow a rising traverse across the face following snow and then rock. Shortly before joining the ridge, head directly up a rock chimney to reach the summit ridge, which is followed back right to the summit.

Descent: Same, using rappels; or follow the summit ridge back north toward the main summit and rappel down to the col before descending via easy ground back to the moraine.

SOUTHEAST RIDGE ROUTE

Grade IV (5.8)/D+ (V), 70°, 700 m/2,300 ft, 6 hours from high camp

DECEMBER 28, 1993, OSWALDO ALCÓCER, OSWALDO FREIRE, AND GABRIEL LLANO (ECUADOR)

Depending on conditions, this can be an unstable rock wall crowned by loose ice and snow. Access the ridge via the south face, sometimes including a 45-m/150-ft vertical pitch on bad rock, and then follow the

ANTISANA PICO SUR
FROM THE NORMAL ROUTE

SOUTHEAST RIDGE ROUTE

FIGURE S ROUTE

southeast ridge to reach the summit, finishing up 65° seracs.

Descent: Figure S Route

TRAVERSE

Grade III/AD+, 50°, 1,100 m/3, 600 ft, 2 days

DECEMBER 1997, BERNARD FRANCOU AND HUBERT SÉIMOND (FRANCE) SOLO

Climb the south ridge of Pico Sur to the summit from its base following the easiest line. Follow the double-corniced ridge north toward the Cumbre Máxima and then rappel down over the difficulties to reach the col between Pico Sur and the main summit and camp. On the second day go up and over the main summit and down the other side, descending via the West Face Direct Route.

sincholagua

4,893 m/16,053 ft

FEBRUARY 23, 1880, JEAN ANTOINE AND LOUIS CARREL (ITALY) AND

EDWARD WHYMPER (U.K.)

Map: Sincholagua

This mountain, just north of the Cotopaxi National Park, is a fun acclimatization peak—as Edward Whymper put it, "something with dash and go" (*Travels,* 1892). The approach and the summit give fantastic views of Cotopaxi, and on a clear day it is possible to see the Ilinizas, Sangay, El Altar, Antisana, and Cotacachi.

The name for this mountain comes from the Quichua word *sinchijahua,* which means "strong above."

Sincholagua was glaciated when Whymper climbed the mountain. Another feature that has changed since his time is the size of the Río Pita, which is now a stream. When Whymper crossed it in 1880 it measured 60 m/200 ft across and 1 m/3 ft deep, but "it was clear that when it was at its highest this stream must have been about 1100 feet wide, and no less than fifty feet deep" (*Travels,* 1892). The reason for this change is that the course of the Río Pita was carved out by the lahar from Cotopaxi's last major eruption in 1877.

ACCESS AND APPROACH

(See the Sincholagua, Rumiñahui, Cotopaxi, and Quilindaña map.)

Note: If you are planning to drive up Sincholagua as far as possible, check with Quito agencies about the current state of the gate at the Río Pita.

A jeep from Quito can get to about 4,100 m/13,450 ft on Sincholagua, passing the trig point 3944. There is excellent but waterless camping a few minutes higher following the track up the ridge.

A pickup hired in Lasso can get to the Río Pita and, in dry conditions,

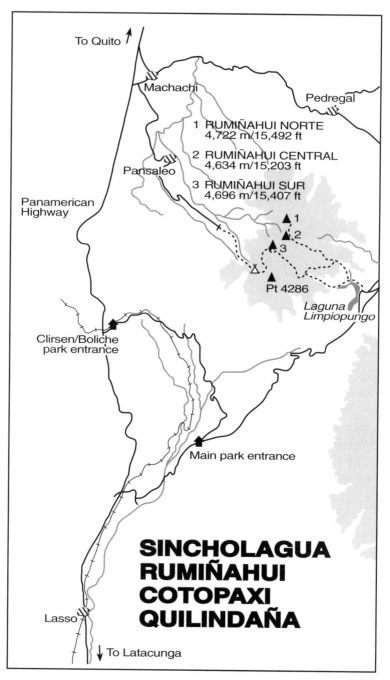

To Quito

Machachi

Pedregal

1 RUMIÑAHUI NORTE
4,722 m/15,492 ft

2 RUMIÑAHUI CENTRAL
4,634 m/15,203 ft

3 RUMIÑAHUI SUR
4,696 m/15,407 ft

Pansaleo

Panamerican
Highway

1
2
3

Pt 4286

Laguna
Limpiopungo

Clirsen/Boliche
park entrance

Main park entrance

**SINCHOLAGUA
RUMIÑAHUI
COTOPAXI
QUILINDAÑA**

Lasso

To Latacunga

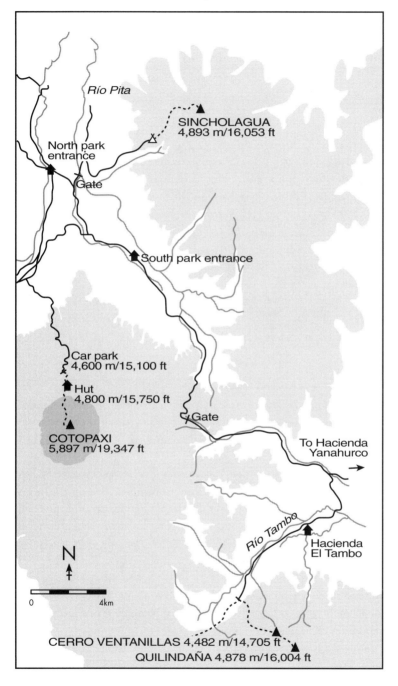

Río Pita

SINCHOLAGUA
4,893 m/16,053 ft

North park
entrance

Gate

South park entrance

Car park
4,600 m/15,100 ft

Hut
4,800 m/15,750 ft

COTOPAXI
5,897 m/19,347 ft

Gate

To Hacienda
Yanahurco

Río Tambo

Hacienda
El Tambo

N

0   4km

CERRO VENTANILLAS 4,482 m/14,705 ft
QUILINDAÑA 4,878 m/16,004 ft

a good way along the track, but the driver is unlikely to know the way. From the Panamerican Highway, use the main entrance to the Cotopaxi National Park, pay the US$10 entrance fee (even though Sincholagua is outside the park), and follow the road. Beyond Limpiopungo a sign points right to Refugio José F. Ribas (the Cotopaxi hut). Turn left and continue to the north park entrance. Immediately before the entrance building, cross the river (by bridge if it is in condition or drive through the river) and turn right. Follow the track down toward the Río Pita and make a switchback turn left above the river valley to reach a sometimes-locked gate and some abandoned buildings. If possible, pass through the gate, pass through the next gate, and cross the Río Pita. Shortly afterward a track heads off to the right. Follow it, cross a stream, rise up on the other side, and then look to leave the track by going rightward to cross a patch of grass and pine trees with a clear track leading up into the *páramo*. Follow the track to the end.

Note: The closest water to the end of the track is in the valley down right—a fair walk.

NORMAL ROUTE

Scramble, the finish is Grade (5.4)/III, 70°, 20 m/60 ft, 3½ hours

Continue along the waterless ridge. When the path drops to a broad col on the ridge, drop right and follow the indistinct path that passes on the right the three small and one big rock outcrops on the ridge before reaching the end of the ridge (1 hour).

From the end of the ridge, head straight up to a rock outcrop, go left under it, and then up the left side. Continue following the intermittent path and cairns trending up and left, going around the back of the first summit. The route starts to become more of a scramble here. Once behind the first summit, follow a falling traverse to reach the valley bottom below the headwall ridge (2 hours).

Follow a rising traverse away from the headwall with trickier scrambling to reach the start of an unpleasantly loose gully. Climb the gully for 10 m/30 ft (5.4/III) to reach another 10 m/30 ft of solid though exposed rock to reach the summit (30 minutes).

Descent: Rappel 25 m/80 ft from the summit to the bottom of the gully. The return to the end of the drivable track takes 2 hours.

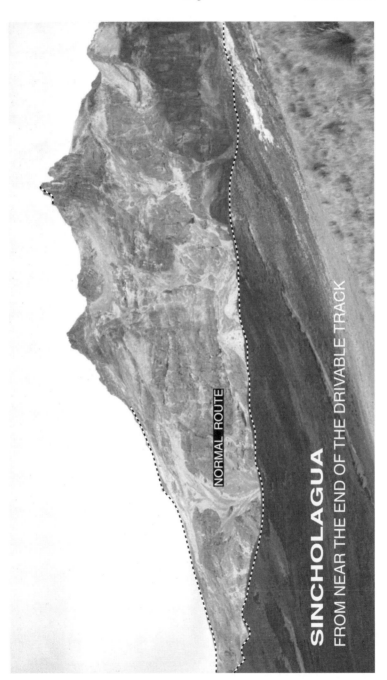

NORMAL ROUTE

SINCHOLAGUA
FROM NEAR THE END OF THE DRIVABLE TRACK

NORMAL DIRECT ROUTE

From the end of the ridge, head up to the rock outcrop, go up the left side, and then continue straight up. Follow a rightward rising traverse to reach a col, with the first summit on the left and the main summit on the right. Drop down the headwall and then follow a rising traverse to the base of the loose gully to rejoin the Normal Route.

Descent: Normal Route

rumiñahui

4,722 m/15,492 ft

THE FIRST ASCENT IS NOT RECORDED.

Maps: Machachi, Sincholagua

(*Note:* The IGM 3rd edition Machachi map misnames all Rumiñahui peaks. The peak marked "Volcán Rumiñahui 4722" is Rumiñahui Norte. The peak to the south marked "4634" is Rumiñahui Central and the peak southwest of this, marked "4696," is Rumiñahui Sur.)

Rumiñahui is made up of three peaks, all of which make good acclimatization climbs—as long as you don't attempt climbing them in one day from Quito. They all present the opportunity for fantastic views of Cotopaxi, which lies to the south. Rumiñahui is a huge caldera open to the northwest and is named after Atahualpa's most famous general who led the fight against the conquistadores after Atahualpa was murdered. In Quichua the name means "stone face."

RUMIÑAHUI CENTRAL AND RUMIÑAHUI NORTE

Central: 4,634 m/15,203 ft

Norte: 4,722 m/15,492 ft

These two peaks are approached from Laguna Limpiopungo in the Cotopaxi National Park and it is quite possible to do Rumiñahui Central and Norte in the same day.

Access

(See the Sincholagua, Rumiñahui, Cotopaxi, and Quilindaña map.)

Note: Camping is prohibited at Laguna Limpiopungo.

Follow the access directions to Cotopaxi and get out at Limpiopungo, or take a bus to Lasso on the Panamerican Highway and hire a pickup to Limpiopungo. Jeep hire from Quito is US$100 for up to four people, US$25 for each additional person up to nine.

NORTE

SUR

CENTRAL

CENTRAL AND NORTE ROUTES

ROUTE FROM LIMPIOPUNGO

RUMIÑAHUI
FROM ABOVE LIMPIOPUNGO

Approach

Follow the path along the right (eastern) edge of Laguna Limpiopungo. After 10 minutes, the path drops slightly to the green plain and crosses a stream. Rise up on the other side and then turn right and look for the path that goes up, staying above and on the left side of the stream until you reach a large green area free of *páramo* grass (30 minutes).

Continue straight on and up to the top of the green area (10 minutes). Carry on up to a broad col and then bear left following the path as it goes between two hills and then up. Go up right to join the ridge 30 minutes from the green area.

Turn left and follow the ridge to reach the first rocky outcrop (20 minutes).

RUMIÑAHUI CENTRAL ROUTE

Follow the path as it goes to the right side of the ridge and then rises, crossing a large scree slope. Head up the right side of the scree slope to the summit (1 hour).

Descent: Go straight down the scree slope to reach the path and then follow it back to the rocky outcrop (30 minutes). From the outcrop, it is 1 hour back to Limpiopungo.

RUMIÑAHUI NORTE ROUTE

Note: A helmet plus rappel gear is necessary for this climb.

Follow the path, cross the large scree slope below Rumiñahui Central, and follow a traverse aiming for a col to the left of a striking lump of rock. From the col, head up left aiming for a narrow gully. Go up on the left side of the gully to reach an exposed step across the gully a couple of meters below the ridge. Cross the gully and then scramble up to the ridge and follow it on the left (northern) side until you reach a steep gully going down left. Rappel 20 m/65 ft down the steep gully, leave the rope in place, and climb back up a less steep but looser gully on the other side and continue up to the summit (2 hours).

Descent: Same. Scramble back down the loose gully and climb up the steep gully using the rope for protection. It takes 1 hour to get back to the rock outcrop and another hour to reach Limpiopungo.

RUMIÑAHUI SUR

4,696 m/15,407 ft

The third of the Rumiñahui peaks is better approached from the north. It is possible to climb Rumiñahui Sur from Machachi and then descend to Limpiopungo in the same day.

Access via Machachi

Take a bus to Machachi (see the access directions to Ilinizas) and then hire a pickup to Pansaleo (15 minutes, less than US$10). The road out of Machachi goes from near the stadium where there is a signpost for Hacienda San Antonio. In Pansaleo, the IGM map shows the main road as a continuation of the road from Machachi. This is wrong. Shortly after the Escuela Kiwanis in Pansaleo there is a purple house on the right, and 100 m/109 yd farther there is a turnoff to the right. Take it. In dry conditions with a four-wheel-drive vehicle it is possible to drive for 5 km/3 mi (15 minutes) up the road to about 3,650 m/11,975 ft where there is a half-bridge over a stream.

Approach

(See the Sincholagua, Rumiñahui, Cotopaxi, and Quilindaña map.)

From the half-bridge, cross the stream and follow the track to the end (1¼ hours). Follow a good path to reach a polylepis wood and excellent camping (15 minutes)—there is a stream near the top end of the wood, heading toward Point 4286. Head off left from the good path and proceed toward the ridge (35 minutes).

From the ridge above the polylepis wood, contour across the scree and rock heading for a cleft to the left of a large pinnacle on the next ridge, which comes down from the south peak running parallel to the ridge down from the central peak. Scramble up the cleft to reach the ridge itself (45 minutes).

NORMAL ROUTE

Scramble up the ridge for 10 m/30 ft and then traverse left into a gully. Scramble up the gully and continue up over scree and rock with some short sections where it is necessary to scramble. The summit is marked by a 3-m-/10-ft-high conglomerate rock—it is necessary to climb up for those summit shots (1½ hours).

Descent: Same

Access and Approach via Limpiopungo

See the approach directions for Ruminahui Central and Norte above until you reach the large green area. Head up and then follow the path going left (west). Follow this path down into the valley between the central and southern spurs and up on the other side and onto the ridge coming down from Ruminahui Sur.

Alternatively, from Limpiopungo, follow the path and then instead of heading up right after crossing the stream, continue around the top end of the plain above the lake and then enter the next valley. Head up onto paths on the left side of what becomes the ridge down from Ruminahui Sur.

Whichever way you go, join the ridge coming down from Ruminahui Sur and follow it up. Just before the first rocky outcrop on the ridge, the path drops to the right before contouring and then rising. About 20 minutes after the outcrop you will come to a second large gully on the left. The gully is full of scree and has a cave on the right side. Head up the left side of the gully to reach the ridge and then follow the route as described above.

Descent: Same

cotopaxi

5,897 m/19,347 ft

NOVEMBER 27–28, 1872, ANGEL MARÍA ESCOBAR (COLOMBIA) AND WILHELM REISS

(GERMANY) FROM THE WEST

Maps: Sincholagua for Normal Route and approach, Cotopaxi for summit and all other routes

Cotopaxi is the most popular mountain in Ecuador and the Andes and justifiably so. It is without doubt one of the most beautiful mountains in the world. Cotopaxi is as perfect as Mount Fuji, but twice as big: the base is 22 km/14 mi across. An added attraction is that statistically Cotopaxi has more clear days than any other of Ecuador's Big Ten, so you have more chance of appreciating its beauty. In Quichua, the name means "necklace of the moon," or "mountain of moonlight."

Cotopaxi is not, as is often stated, the highest active volcano in the world, even using Arturo Eichler's old height of 6,005 m/19,701 ft. There are a number of higher active volcanoes in Chile near the Bolivian border, including Guallatiri 6,071 m/19,918 ft. At the top of Cotopaxi, you can see sulfur fumaroles in the crater, which measures 800 m/2,600 ft north-south and 640 m/2,100 ft east-west. The first descent to the crater was in 1972 by a Czechoslovak-Polish expedition complete with gas masks.

Vulcanologists use remote seismic sensors and incredibly accurate global positioning systems (GPS) equipment to monitor the mountain's shape and size—indicators of increased volcanic activity. The mountain has erupted on average every 100 to 120 years with the last big eruption in 1877—it could go up again next week (with some warning) or not for another century or two. Vulcanologists say the disappearance and reappearance of glaciers, especially on the western side, is because of climatic rather than volcanic factors.

Baron Max von Thielmann, writing in the *Alpine Journal* (1876–78), states that "The whole thing is but an inclined snow, pretty steep (about 40°), but without the slightest difficulty or danger . . . we reached the summit with the greatest ease." While Cotopaxi is technically not challenging, it must be remembered that the glacier is covered with innumerable crevasses in which climbers are killed every year.

ACCESS
(See the Sincholagua, Rumiñahui, Cotopaxi, and Quilindaña map.)

The entrances to the Cotopaxi National Park are open 7 A.M. to 3 P.M. (exit until 6 P.M.) daily and cost US$10 per person.

Normal access: From Quito's Terminal Terrestre, take a bus to Lasso or a bus going to any point farther south (for example, Latacunga or Riobamba). In Lasso, hire a pickup to the hut car park at 4,600 m/ 15,100 ft (2½ hours, US$40).

A jeep from Quito takes 1½ hours to the exit from the Panamerican Highway and another 1½ hours to the car park. The transport costs US$100 for up to four people, US$20 for each additional person up to nine.

Looking down into the active Cotopaxi crater from the summit

Access via the north park entrance: This is a rarely used but beautiful route that requires a four-wheel-drive vehicle. The road climbs out
of the town of Machachi on the Panamerican Highway, passes through
Pedregal, enters the park, and then continues more or less south to join
the normal road coming in from the west at Limpiopungo and goes up
to the car park.

APPROACH

From the car park at 4,600 m/15,100 ft, head up to the hut following
the zigzag path to the left. (The path straight up is loose stuff and far
better left for the descent.) Even though you can see the hut from the
car park, it still takes 45 minutes to get there.

The hut is at 4,800 m/15,750 ft and is the most popular in Ecuador, not
just for climbers but also for Ecuadorians who go up to party, especially
on weekends and holidays (Christmas, New Year's, Carnival, Easter, and
so forth). As a result, it is noisy, dirty, and crowded—the record number
of people to spend the night in the hut is 118. The toilets, when open,
are bucket-flushed. Sleep is difficult. For this pleasure, you pay US$10
per person per night. As a result, increasing numbers of people are
choosing to camp up to the left of the hut.

NORMAL ROUTE

Grade II/PD, 50°, 1,100 m/3,600 ft, 5–8 hours

SEPTEMBER 9, 1877, JOSÉ SANDOVAL (ECUADOR) AND TEODORO WOLF (GERMANY)

From the hut, follow the path going past the toilet block and up the
rock/scree ridge on the right of the triangular red scree slope, which
can be snow-covered. Follow the path up, zigzagging through the scree
or snow to the top to reach the glacier (1¼ hours).

Access to the glacier changes from season to season. Sometimes it is
straight up; sometimes it is to the right. The route stays on or beyond
the ridge to the right of the icefall coming down from Yanasacha (Black
Rock), aiming for the right side of Yanasacha. There is a sheltered spot
to the right of Yanasacha (2½ hours from the start of the glacier).

From the sheltered spot, traverse right for 200 m/650 ft and then
head up diagonally left on steeper ground (up to 50°). There can be a
large crevasse to deal with 30 minutes from Yanasacha. This was bridged
in early 1998, although it became necessary to drop into the crevasse,

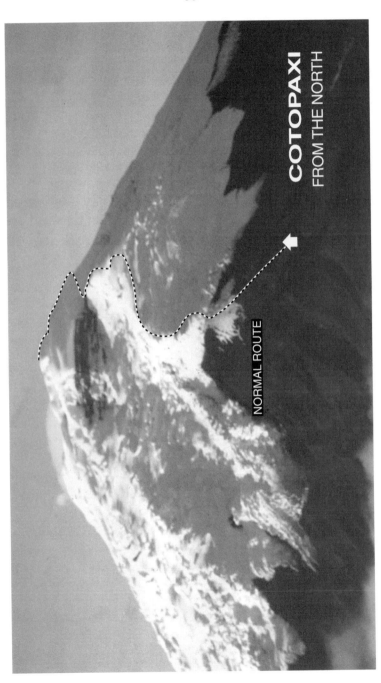

COTOPAXI
FROM THE NORTH

NORMAL ROUTE

follow it along the bottom, and then climb the bridge and steep (60°) ground to exit. Above the crevasse, head straight up to the crater rim and turn left, following the rim to reach the highest point (30 minutes). If the crevasse is not crossable, it is necessary to continue the traverse from Yanasacha for a longer time before heading up to the crater rim, turning left, and then continuing to the summit. This takes up to 2 hours longer from Yanasacha than the more direct route.

Descent: Same (2 to 3 hours). At the foot of the glacier, head right and take a more direct route back to the hut down the scree.

OUTER CRATER CIRCUIT

Grade III+/AD, 55°, 4–8 hours

JUNE 14–16, 1976, MINARD "PETE" HALL (U.S.) AND MARTIN SLATER (U.K.)

Follow the Normal Route to the ice cliff shelter to the right of Yanasacha and camp. Continue following the Normal Route to the summit and then walk around the outer rim of the crater.

INNER RING CIRCUIT

Grade III/AD-, 50°, 2 hours

This route is quicker than the Outer Crater Circuit. Immediately upon reaching the crater, head right and drop down to the inner snow ring. Follow this all the way around.

OTHER ROUTES

Being virtually symmetrical, Cotopaxi can be climbed from any direction. Choice of alternative routes depends on how far you are prepared to walk. The first and second ascents of Cotopaxi were from the southwest. Teodoro Wolf (Germany) and José Sandoval (Ecuador) were the first to climb from Limpiopungo in September 1877, three months after the huge eruption of June 1877, and they followed the northwest lava flow to Yanasacha—essentially, the current Normal Route. Until the hut was opened in 1971, Cotopaxi was normally climbed from the southwest. Nicolás Martínez climbed from the east in 1912.

quilindaña

4,878 m/16,004 ft

FEBRUARY 23, 1952, ARTURO EICHLER (GERMANY), JUAN ELIZALDE (ECUADOR),

PAUL FERET (FRANCE), HORACIO LÓPEZ (COLOMBIA), FRANCO ANZIL,

GIOVANNI VERGANI, AND ALFONSO VINCI (ITALY)

Maps: For access from the north, use Cotopaxi plus Sincholagua if you want to cover the way through the Cotopaxi National Park. For access from the south, use Cotopaxi, Mulaló, Latacunga (restricted), and Laguna de Anteojos.

The "Matterhorn of Ecuador" lies 17 km/11 mi southwest of Cotopaxi and is higher than Mont Blanc. On a good day you might see it from the summit of Cotopaxi where it appears to be a pretty evil-looking lump of rock out in the *páramo*, but otherwise it tends to remain out of view.

Allegedly, the name comes from the words *qui* (to make or do), *lin* (male), *ta* (cylindrical thing), and *ña* (company), which translates to something like "to be male this cylindrical thing that accompanies." Apart from not making sense, this description has nothing to do with the shape of the mountain.

ACCESS

(See the Sincholagua, Rumiñahui, Cotopaxi, and Quilindaña map.)

There are two access routes north and south. The south access, while appearing more logical and used by the first ascenders, is via far worse roads, and in all but the driest of conditions is difficult. The northern access is longer and involves paying to enter the Cotopaxi National Park, but it is far more secure in terms of road conditions. For both access routes you need permission from the relevant landowners and a key to pass through the relevant gates operated by Fundación Páramo (contact Juan Fernando or Jorge Pérez in Quito, tel 444429) in the north and Hacienda Baños in the south.

ACCESS FROM THE NORTH

Follow the access directions for Cotopaxi, proceed to the main Cotopaxi park entrance. Pay the US$10 entrance fee and follow the signs for Refugio José F. Ribas until after Laguna Limpiopungo where there is a sign pointing right for the refugio and straight on for the "Sitio Arqueológico." Go straight on and keep following the signs for the Sitio Arqueológico. When you come down to the plain on the northeastern side of Cotopaxi, stay right and about 45 minutes after entering the park you will arrive at the abandoned and vandalized south park entrance. Thirty minutes later you will reach the very solid and very locked gate operated by Fundacíon Páramo. From here it is another 30 minutes to the signposted left turn heading to Hacienda Yanahurco. Go straight on through the wooden gate to enter the Hacienda El Tambo valley. There are three stream crossings before you reach the hacienda 10 minutes later. Pass through the two gates of the hacienda and continue up the faint track until you reach another wooden gate in 20 minutes at about 3,800 m/12,500 ft. It is not worth trying to take a four-wheel-drive vehicle farther than this point.

Jeep hire from Quito is US$140 for up to four people, US$35 for each additional person up to nine.

APPROACH

Go through the gate and follow the broad green swath uphill through the *páramo* until you are opposite Cerro Ventanillas at 4,482 m/14,705 ft and then head straight for the hill. Camping is possible at various points. It takes 3 hours to reach Ventanillas, which overlooks Quilindaña.

NORTHWEST RIDGE NORMAL ROUTE

Grade (5.7)/(V), 400 m/1,300 ft, 4 hours

Find a way up onto the ridge and follow it to the summit. You will encounter technical sections before the route finishes as a scramble to the summit.

Descent: Same, using rappels.

hermoso (yurac llanganati)

4,571 m/14,997 ft

1941, CARLOS HIRTZ, DMITRI KAKABADSE, GEORG KIEDERLE, AND TONI STUISS (GERMANY)

Maps: Sucre (and San José de Paoló if coming in from the north)

The Llanganates range, of which Hermoso is the highest peak, is wild and wet. Very wet.

Michael Koerner, who declined to enter the area, wrote: "The Llanganates are a mysterious and almost impenetrable range to the NE of Baños. Part of Atahualpa's gold is said to be hidden there, and people occasionally go off to look for it. You can too if your interest is to get hideously and hopelessly lost in 15 foot high, razor sharp pampas grass and continous rain.

"The Langanates also contain El Hermoso, 4571 m, an occasional snow peak, the identity of which will baffle you when first you see it from some other peak" (*Fool's Climbing Guide*, 1976).

The tale behind the gold runs as follows: When the Spanish arrived in South America they captured the Inca ruler Atahualpa at Cusco in modern-day Peru. Atahualpa tried to buy himself out of captivity and promised to supply the Spaniards with more gold than they could imagine. The gold was brought in from all parts of the Inca empire, but the Spanish decided they had enough and Atahualpa was garroted. One consignment of gold, estimated at 750 tons, was in transit from Quito when the news came that Atahualpa was dead. The Inca general in charge of this gold, Rumiñahui, decided to hide it and so, it is said, chose the Llanganates where the treasure was hidden in 1533.

This might have been the end of the matter except in the eighteenth century a Spanish mercenary called Valverde married an Indian woman in Latacunga whose father promised the Spaniard huge amounts of wealth. The soldier became rich, moved back to Spain, and when he

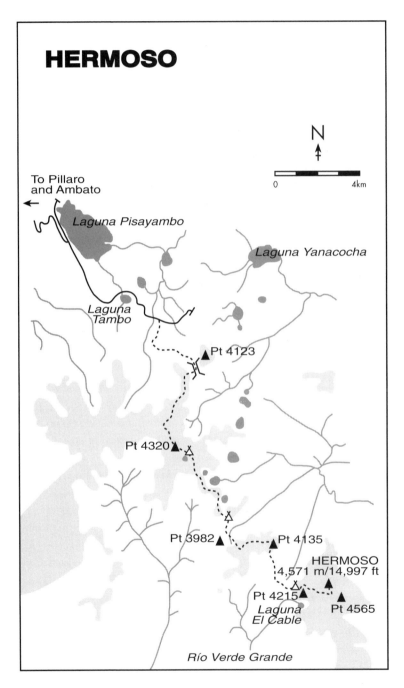

HERMOSO

N

0   4km

To Pillaro
and Ambato

Laguna Pisayambo

Laguna Yanacocha

Laguna
Tambo

Pt 4123

Pt 4320

Pt 3982   Pt 4135

HERMOSO
4,571 m/14,997 ft

Pt 4215
Laguna
El Cable   Pt 4565

Río Verde Grande

Cerro Hermoso rising out of the clouds in the mysterious Llanganates

died sent a description of how to find the gold to the King of Spain, who immediately ordered the first of many unsuccessful searches for the treasure. The lure of untold riches still attracts adventurers to search for the gold, including George Dyott (who looked for Colonel Fawcett after his disappearance) and climbers Hamish MacInnes, Joe Brown, and Yvon Chouinard. The Swiss-German Eugene Brunner, who accompanied Dyott, spent forty-two years looking for the gold. On one trip he saw the sun only once in 127 days. MacInnes, who went in three times, described the area "as inaccessible as anywhere on earth, where mist, dense as glass fibre, obliterates the mountains for months on end" (*Beyond the Ranges: Five Years in the Life of Hamish MacInnes*, 1984).

To be fully equipped you need the following items: maps, waterproof map case, compass or GPS, machete, galoshes, *salopettes,* dry bags for storing everything, a tent with a separate fly so that the inside can be kept dry, a spare set of clothes.

Leaving early from Pillaro, a strong party could climb Hermoso and get back to the road on the fourth day. If you are not going so strong, however, plan on 5 days. Arrange a pick up as well as a drop off—it is a long way out along the road.

ACCESS

Traditionally, access to the Llanganates has been from Triunfo 2,500 m/ 8,200 ft, the starting point of Valverde's gold trail description. Depending on conditions, from Triunfo it takes 6 hours following the Río Verde Chico to reach camp at Rancho Grande and then another 8 hours to reach camp at Laguna Brunner.

A better alternative is to go in from Pillaro in the north because you start higher (3,650 m/11,970 ft) and stay high, thereby remaining, on the whole, in *páramo* where the visibility and routefinding is easier than in densely vegetated areas.

From the north via Pillaro: From Quito's Terminal Terrestre to Pillaro by bus takes 3 hours and costs US$2.20. There are three buses a day Monday to Saturday and none on Sunday. Alternatively, take a bus to Ambato and then take another bus to Pillaro.

Pillaro has two hotels and a number of basic eateries. Market day is Thursday when there is plenty of transport to the town and a lot of pick-ups waiting to take you farther up the road. In the Pillaro square, arrange a pickup for the 1½-hour journey up to the end of the road past the Pisayambo Dam (US$30). The road up can give fantastic views but rides are better in the early morning, so get to Pillaro the night before and organize the transport for first thing in the morning.

APPROACH

There are many trails in the Llanganates made by animals and treasure hunters. The quality depends on the season and how recently someone went through with a machete. It is easy to lose the trail, and some just peter out. Not all of them go where you want to. In addition, low cloud cover reduces visibility to under 30 m/100 ft, so it is essential to know where you are on the map at all times.

From the road at grid reference 945765, follow paths to the left of the waterfall and up to a saddle at 963743 to the right/southeast of Point 4123 in 1½ hours. In good visibility you can see the next saddle to the south where there is good camping above the lake around 956708.

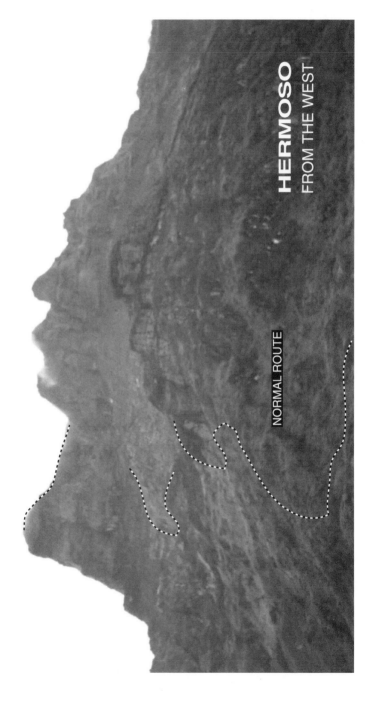

HERMOSO
FROM THE WEST

NORMAL ROUTE

Getting to it is not so easy. Either drop down and then go up the boggy valley or follow the ridge to behind Point 4320 and drop down following cattle paths to arrive just below the saddle. Both alternatives take about 4 hours from the first saddle.

From the saddle, take a bearing on Point 3982 and then follow the right side of the ridge before following the ridge itself to reach a boggy but flat area after 1 hour. Follow the ridge and, when it joins the next hill, traverse leftward staying well above the lake. The trail then rises to ideal camping near a pond at 975679 in 1½ hours.

Drop down to a broad saddle at 974673. When you reach the flat part of the saddle and a small pond surrounded by bog, head off diagonally left and down aiming for some vegetation-covered rock. Go up the rock and then head left to reach two small shallow ponds in 1 hour. Follow the ridge to Point 4135 and then drop south and follow the ridge to 000650 in another hour. In clear weather this ridge gives fantastic views of Cerro Hermoso. At the end of the ridge, drop east to the saddle at 002649. From here it takes about 1 hour to head up east toward Point 4215; it is possible to camp at a number of places depending on how much bog you are prepared to sleep in.

NORMAL ROUTE

The idea is to get into the valley between the highest peak (the left or northern peak) and its right (southern) neighbor Point 4565, scramble up to the ridge linking the two, turn left, and follow the ridge to the summit. The route takes 3 hours from camp below Point 4215.

From camp, head up until you reach a rock wall. A path goes right, but it is quicker to go left. When you arrive at the eastern side of Point 4215, head for the gap between the two main peaks.

Descent: Same; 1½ hours.

tungurahua

5,016 m/16,456 ft

FEBRUARY 8, 1873, WILHELM REISS AND ALPHONS STÜBEL (GERMANY),

EUSEBIO RODRÍGUEZ (COLOMBIA), JOSÉ REYES AND OTHER ECUADORIANS

VIA BAÑOS AND COCHA DE SAN PABLO

Map: Baños

Despite warnings, two Australian climbers and a local guide became the last people to attempt to climb Tungurahua on October 5, 1999. All three were hospitalized, and the civil defense immediately declared the mountain "off limits." The volcano had been on Yellow Alert since September 1999, and it was upgraded to Orange Alert in October following a series of explosions.

Tungurahua has a history of violent eruptions, and vulcanologists have advised that the cycle seems to be approximately every one hundred years. The previous eruption was in 1916, and although activity reinitiated after only eighty-three years, it is still within their parameters. Baños and other nearby towns and villages were evacuated on October 17, 1999, and since that date explosions and eruptions have been carefully monitored. Incandescent rocks and hot ashfall has caused some melting of snow and ice. Although much of the glacier has been covered with ash, vulcanologists believe that the majority of it still remains, presenting the potential hazard of mudflows and lahars. The road between Riobamba and Baños is already impassible as a result of various slides.

Tungurahua has now become a major tourist attraction, with four principal sites from which to watch the nightly activity: to the north, at Ojos del Volcan and Chontilla, to the west at Cotaló, and in the south at Cerro Arrayan. All the sites face the volcano and are approximately 10 kilometers distant from the activity.

Some residents of Baños forced their way back into the town at the beginning of the year 2000 and informed authorities that they were not prepared to continue camping out in churches, schools, and other buildings in neighboring towns. The civil and military authorities met with

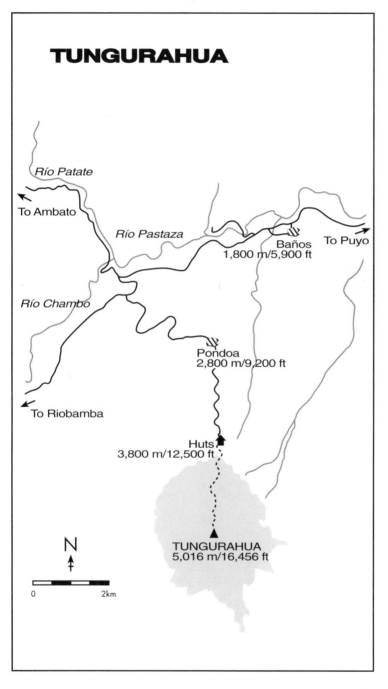

TUNGURAHUA

Río Patate

To Ambato

Río Pastaza

Baños
1,800 m/5,900 ft

To Puyo

Río Chambo

Pondoa
2,800 m/9,200 ft

To Riobamba

Huts
3,800 m/12,500 ft

N

0   2km

TUNGURAHUA
5,016 m/16,456 ft

vulcanologists and decided that it was far too difficult to keep people out. However, they issued strong warnings and have stated that they will not be responsible for rescue services or accidents within the area. They plan to put up signs explaining the dangers on all approaches to Baños.

ACCESS

Note: Arrangements are expected to be the same as those listed here after the current eruptive phase ends.

Take a bus from Quito's Terminal Terrestre to Baños (3½ hours, US$3). Spend the night in Baños, a pleasant resort town, and catch the milk truck that leaves daily around 9 A.M. from outside Pension Patty on Calle Eloy Alfaro between Ambato and Oriente and take it to the park entrance in Pondoa (1 hour, US$2 per person). The truck returns to Baños daily between midday and 2 P.M.

Alternatively, hire a pickup from the Cooperativa Agoyan on the Parque Central, Calle Maldonado (US$12 for up to five people), or hire a jeep from one of the Baños agencies.

Tungurahua from the higher huts

Jeep hire from Quito to Pondoa is US$140 for up to four people, US$35 for each additional person up to nine.

Note: At the time of this writing there were no ASEGUIM guides based in Baños. The best guide is Willie Navarrete. Guiding and equipment can be of dangerously low quality when organized in Baños.

APPROACH

It is possible to hire horses (US$5 to $7 each) to go from the park entrance in Pondoa to the huts. The investment is well worth it given the 1,000 m/3,300 ft of ascent.

Register with the Parque Nacional Sangay park guard and pay the US$10 entrance. Walk up the

NORMAL ROUTE

TUNGURAHUA
FROM ABOVE THE HUTS

road for 50 m/165 ft and then turn left and follow the clear and often-used path up to the huts, passing through tunnels made of bamboo and other plants. In wet conditions this trek is a nightmare with sections of inescapable knee-deep mud. It takes 3 to 4 hours to reach the huts at 3,800 m/12,500 ft. Tungurahua is not a good choice as an acclimatization climb.

The lower hut is newer, bigger, and better and costs US$3.50 per night. Basic cooking facilities and floor space are also available for US$3 per night at the higher hut. None of them are particularly safe to leave things in and you need a sleeping mat.

Warning: All water collected from near the higher hut should be boiled or treated with iodine because of the amount of human feces around the huts contaminating all available water.

NORMAL ROUTE

Grade I/F, 35°, 1,200 m/3,900 ft, 4–6 hours

Join the north ridge behind the huts and follow the well-worn path through the vegetation and up to a small concrete hut that marks the boundary of the Sangay National Park. Slowly zigzag up the scree, following the path that eventually cuts left to join a rocky ridge that returns to scree before arriving at the glacier at around 4,900 m/16,075 ft. Pass the fumaroles, rope up for the glacier—there are crevasses—and plod up to the summit in 30 minutes.

Descent: Same, but much quicker; 2 hours to the huts. It is easy enough to return to Baños the same day.

CRATER CIRCUIT

AUGUST 23, 1981, REMIGIO GALÁRRAGA, JORGE GUANO, GERMÁN LUNA, AND IVÁN VALLEJO (ECUADOR)

Tick all seven peaks, starting with the first one to the north of the highest peak, heading south to climb the highest peak, and then continuing on, climbing rock (4 hours).

SOUTHWEST FLANK/SOUTH RIDGE ROUTE

FEBRUARY 26, 1989, PABLO CATALÁN AND ALFREDO MENSI (ECUADOR)

el altar

Maps: Volcán El Altar, Palitahua

This mountain group presents the hardest climbing in Ecuador. El Altar is an old volcano with the west side blown out, leaving a crescent 3 km/1.75 mi across with nine peaks. It looks remarkably similar to the post-1980 Mount St. Helens, which lost 1,000 m/3,300 ft of height from what was its summit to what is now the bottom of its crater. Similarly, El Altar was 500 m/1,600 ft to 1,000 m/3,300 ft higher—higher than Cotopaxi—before it collapsed during an eruption.

A legend says that El Altar tried to steal Tungurahua, Chimborazo's wife. Chimborazo went to war against El Altar and won, leaving El Altar smashed. According to Indian legend, the collapse happened in 1460; geologists say the collapse happened a lot earlier. Both the original names for El Altar, in Quichua Capac Urcu and in Aymara Collana, mean "almighty" or "magnificent" mountain, indicating the collapse happened relatively recently. The Spanish named the remains of the mountain El Altar, likening it to a cathedral, and the German explorer and climber Hans Meyer christened the peaks with their individual religious names.

El Altar is made up of nine major summits arranged in a reverse C-shape. Starting with the highest in the south and going around counterclockwise the peaks are as follows: Obispo; Monja Grande; Monja Chica; Tabernáculo; the three Frailes Oriental, Central, and Grande; and Canónigo. Tabernáculo has three summits: north, central, and south (the highest). Another Fraile peak, Beato, is not on El Altar's crater rim but lies on a spur to the east-northeast of Fraile Oriental.

ACCESSES AND APPROACHES

There are two ways in to El Altar depending on whether you want to climb the southern peaks (Obispo and the Monjas) or the northern peaks (Canónigo and the Frailes). To get to the eastern peak of

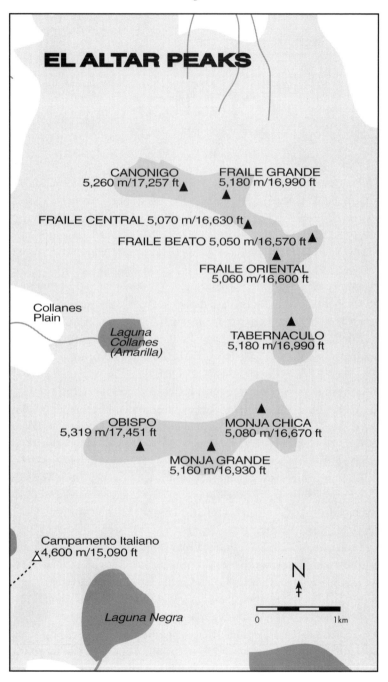

EL ALTAR PEAKS

CANONIGO
5,260 m/17,257 ft ▲

FRAILE GRANDE
5,180 m/16,990 ft ▲

FRAILE CENTRAL 5,070 m/16,630 ft ▲

FRAILE BEATO 5,050 m/16,570 ft ▲

FRAILE ORIENTAL
5,060 m/16,600 ft ▲

Collanes
Plain

*Laguna
Collanes
(Amarilla)*

TABERNACULO
5,180 m/16,990 ft ▲

OBISPO
5,319 m/17,451 ft ▲

MONJA CHICA
5,080 m/16,670 ft ▲

MONJA GRANDE
5,160 m/16,930 ft ▲

Campamento Italiano
△ 4,600 m/15,090 ft

N
↑

Laguna Negra

0   1 km

Tabernáculo, it is farther but easier to approach from the south.

Either way, jeep hire from Quito is US$140 for up to four people; US$35 for each additional person up to nine.

To use public transport for the north or south peaks, take a bus from Quito's Terminal Terrestre to Riobamba (3½ hours, US$3) and then take a taxi to Riobamba's Terminal Oriente (10 minutes, US$1.10).

For Obispo and the southern peaks: From Riobamba's Terminal Oriente there are regular pickup trucks going to Quimiag, but there is little or no transport available in the village to take you farther. It is better to hire a pickup or taxi from the terminal in Riobamba to take you to the end of the road at the Vaquería Inguisay, which is also known locally as Boca Toma 3,550 m/11,650 ft (1¼ hours, US$25). It is possible to camp at the end of the road next to the dam. Horses and mules are available for hire at US$10 per day—ask local *campesinos*. If you arrive in the afternoon, you will be able to leave with animals the next morning.

From the roadhead, cross the small concrete bridge and then go up and through the fenced field on the other side. Enter the field either immediately on the other side of the bridge or 30 m/yd up the track. At the top of the field, join the broad and often muddy track and turn right. The track becomes a path and heads up the left side of the Río Tiaco Chico valley. After 1¼ hours at about 3,700 m/12,150 ft, just below where the Quebrada Tzeles Tiaco joins the Río Tiaco Chico, cross the stream to the right side of the valley. The path then rises up on the right, and after 2 hours you reach a saddle at 4,250 m/13,940 ft. Turn left and follow the path along the ridge for 1¼ hours almost to the Campamento Italiano, a spectacularly sited basecamp area at 4,600 m/ 15,090 ft with water 10 minutes down the right side of the ridge toward the glacier. If the camp is occupied, there are a number of flat dry spots before the Italian Camp where you can camp.

Note: It is not uncommon for muleteers to try to stop 30 minutes from the saddle where there is a short drop, which the animals cannot get down. If this happens, lead the animals back along the path for 30 m/yd and then drop down following a good path that goes around the drop.

For Canónigo and the northern peaks: To save messing around looking for transport farther along the road, hire a pickup or taxi from Riobamba's Terminal Oriente to take you to Hacienda Releche via Penipe and Candelaria (1½ hours, US$25). There is a park entrance

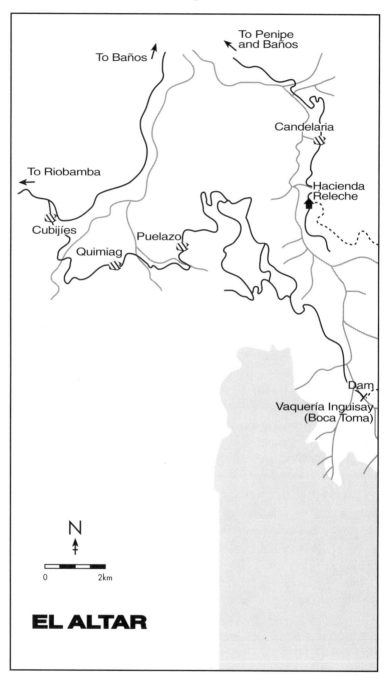

To Baños

To Penipe
and Baños

Candelaria

To Riobamba

Hacienda
Releche

Cubijíes

Puelazo

Quimiag

Dam
Vaquería Inguisay
(Boca Toma)

N

0   2km

EL ALTAR

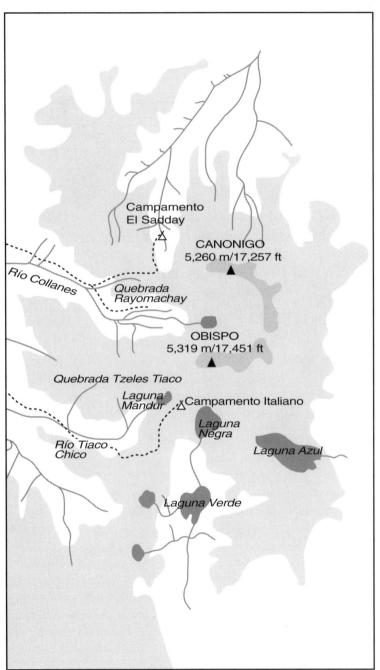

Finishing the gully, Obispo Normal Route, El Altar

office just before the hacienda where you must register and where you will be charged US$10 entrance to Parque Nacional Sangay. It is possible to stay the night at the hacienda guest house and hire horses to the Collanes Plain.

From the hacienda, follow the increasingly clear and often muddy path through fields and up, entering the Río Collanes valley on its left side. There is a three-tent-sized cave 35 minutes before the plain, about 4 hours from Releche, which offers good protection against the rain. Before the cave is a stream, marked Quebrada Rayomachay on the IGM map. Head up left before the stream and stay on the left side of the valley. There used to be a good path and it can be followed intermittently.

Stay on the left side of the bog and continue to the shallow ridge at the other side (2 hours from the main path). Drop down the abandoned path to reach the boggy valley head below surrounded by ten or so waterfalls (20 minutes). There are some drier spots on the other side of the valley where you can camp (3,950 m/12,960 ft). Running water is not a problem.

Note: If you decide to switch camp, from the Collanes Plain up and over the Gampala Ridge to Campamento Italiano takes 6 hours and includes 800 m/2,600 ft of vertical ascent. From the Italian Camp down to the Collanes Plain takes 3 hours. Up or down, you either have to wade the Río Collanes or walk up to the top end of the plain to cross the river where it is less deep.

It is a long walk out to the nearest lift via either Boca Toma or Hacienda Releche—organize a pick up or be prepared for sore knees and feet.

El Altar peaks are divided into southern and northern groupings. They are described starting in the west and going east, with Tabernáculo placed at the end of the southern peaks.

Southern El Altar Peaks

OBISPO

5,319 m/17,451 ft

JULY 7, 1963, FERDINANDO GASPARD, MARINO TREMONTI, AND CLAUDIO ZARDINI (ITALY)

Obispo is the most popular of El Altar's peaks because it is the easiest to get to and the highest. It also has some of the best climbing, which in good conditions is excellent, with the experience further improved by impressive belay views of Sangay to the south.

The choice of which of the three standard ways up Obispo to take depends on snow and ice conditions, as does the difficulty of the route. Access to the Italian Route can be blocked by a bergschrund, or the rock band linking the lower and higher glaciers can be 100 m/330 ft long. If not filled in with snow or ice, the Calvario Route can be steep rock. The icefall is completely unpredictable, but it can be the only non-rock route up.

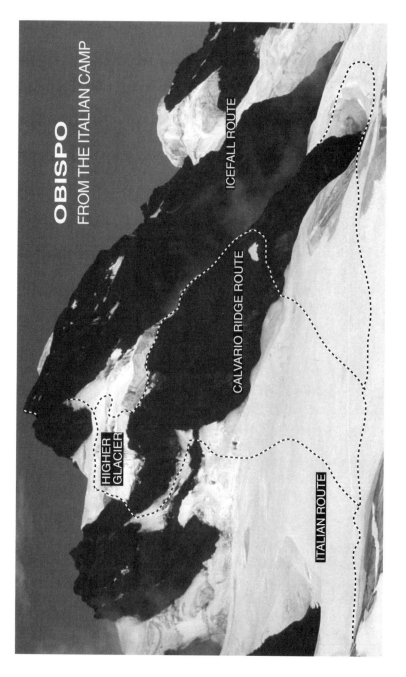

OBISPO
FROM THE ITALIAN CAMP

ICEFALL ROUTE

CALVARIO RIDGE ROUTE

HIGHER GLACIER

ITALIAN ROUTE

ITALIAN ROUTE

Grade IV+ (5.7)/D (V), 80°, 350 m/1,150 ft, 4 hours from the base of the route

JULY 7, 1963, FERDINANDO GASPARD, MARINO TREMONTI, AND CLAUDIO ZARDINI (ITALY)

From Campamento Italiano, descend following the clear path to rock below and then walk up staying to the left to reach the glacier at 4,600 m/ 15,100 ft (20 minutes). Head up and then contour across the glacier until you are below the glacier coming down to the left of Obispo. Go up this glacier to a short rock band (3 m/10 ft) at about 5,000 m/16,400 ft. Climb the rock to reach the base of a steep (70°, 100 m/330 ft) snow gully. Climb the gully to reach a narrow ridge and the higher glacier. Head up over easier ground until you reach a large serac wall. Traverse right under the wall almost to its end and then head up one of several gullies (80°+, 40 m/120 ft) to reach the higher triangular-shaped glacier. Climb the glacier to its apex and then continue up the rock/mud/ snow/ice gully to the summit ridge. Turn right and climb the rock to the summit (5.7/IV, 30 m/100 ft).

Descent: Same, using rappels.

CALVARIO RIDGE ROUTE

Grade IV+ (5.7)/D (V), 80°, 400 m/1,300 ft, 5 hours from the base of the route

This is an alternative way up Obispo for those who like rock climbing. Traverse below the first glacier to reach the rock ridge. Move up onto the ridge and then follow it to reach the higher glacier and join the Italian Route.

Descent: Italian Route

ICEFALL ROUTE

Grade IV/D+, 80°, 450 m/1,480 ft, 7 hours

JANUARY 3, 1990, JULIE AND MATT CULBERSON (U.S.)

Continue west, past the bottom of the Calvario rock ridge, around the end, and head up left to the icefall, which is climbed by the safest line possible. It can be necessary to climb a rock section (5.4/II) to reach the snow/ice to arrive at the base of the summit pyramid. The summit pyramid can be snow and then bad rock or snow all the way.

Descent: Italian Route

NORTH FACE ROUTE

Grade VI (5.9)/ED (VI), 90°+, 800 m/2,600 ft, 4 days

DECEMBER 6–10, 1984, GUILLES DE LATAILLADE (FRANCE) AND OSWALDO MORALES (ECUADOR)

This is the hardest route yet recorded in Ecuador. Poor snow, rock averaging 60°, permanent objective danger from avalanche and rockfall, and four bivouacs are the challenges here. Unrepeated.

Descent: Italian Route

MONJA GRANDE

5,160 m/16,930 ft

AUGUST 17, 1968, BILL ROSS AND MARGARET YOUNG (U.S.)

This is the third highest of El Altar's nine major summits. The approach is none too hard and the climbing satisfyingly challenging to make it worth the effort to climb Monja Grande as well as the more popular Obispo on the same trip.

Approach

From Campamento Italiano it takes 1½ hours to cross the glacier to reach the bottom of the mountain below the col between Obispo and Monja Grande. A camp here will be colder, but it leaves you with a quicker ascent than from Campamento Italiano.

NORMAL ROUTE

Grade IV/D, 80°, 300 m/1,000 ft, 6 hours

Go up the left side of the south glacier, which is very crevassed. The right side is equally crevassed, but it has the additional hazard of huge serac walls above. Work a way up toward the col between Obispo and Monja Grande and then head right to the summit.

Descent: Same, using rappels; 3 hours.

MONJA CHICA

5,080m/16,670ft

JANUARY 16, 1971, PETER BEDNAR, ERICH GRIESSL, GÜNTER HELL, RUDOLF LETTENMEIER, AND SEPP RIESER (GERMANY)

Beyond Monja Grande lie two rarely seen and even more rarely climbed peaks: Monja Chica and Tabernáculo (5,180 m/16,990 ft),

MONJA GRANDE
FROM THE ITALIAN CAMP

NORMAL ROUTE

which was first climbed via the northwest face by the same team that climbed Monja Chica, 3 days later. There is a lot of confusion over the names and heights of the subsidiary Tabernáculo peaks. The Germans climbed Tabernáculo III (Norte) via the southwest face on January 26, 1971. The southernmost peak is believed to be the highest, first climbed via the south face on December 30, 1981, by Fabián Almeida, Fabián Cáceres, Santiago Palacios, and Hernán and Mauricio Reinoso (Ecuador).

Approach

From Campamento Italiano, cross the glaciers below Obispo and Monja Grande. The Monja Grande glacier flattens out to the south. Head down to this part and then across left (west) towards the rock ridge coming south from Monja Grande. Head up, staying to the left of the ridge until there is easy access onto the ridge and camping at 4,750 m/15,580 ft (2 hours). During the day there is plenty of clear water runoff from the glacier.

It is relatively easy to drop down to the broad and relatively flat glacier to the southeast of Monja Chica, but there are some massive crevasses to be avoided.

Major crevasses below Monja Chica, El Altar

Northern El Altar Peaks

CANÓNIGO

5,260 m/17,257 ft

MARCH 7, 1965, FERDINANDO GASPARD, LORENZO LORENZI, MARINO TREMONTI, AND CLAUDIO ZARDINI (ITALY)

This is the second highest of El Altar's peaks, but it has a lot more arduous approach and longer and harder routes than its southern neighbors. For these reasons it is far less popular.

Approach

From the Machay de Cerro Negro cave, continue northeast, cross a boggy area to reach a rocky ridge coming down northwest from Canónigo and either set up camp on the ridge (called Campamento El Sadday or Campamento de la Roca) or cross it and continue dropping down and then heading up right toward the next ridge. Head up before you reach the ridge and set up high camp around 4,600 m/15,100 ft.

ITALIAN ROUTE

Grade V/TD-, 90°, 700 m/2,300 ft, 10 hours

MARCH 7, 1965, FERDINANDO GASPARD, LORENZO LORENZI, MARINO TREMONTI, AND CLAUDIO ZARDINI (ITALY)

From high camp, head up aiming for the eastern (left) summit, and then head right to find an ice-filled overhanging chimney (Grade 5.5/IV, 20 m/65 ft). Carry on up to reach the summit ridge to the east of the main summit, turn right, and follow to the summit.

Descent: Same, using rappels; 5 hours.

THE FRAILES

The four peaks that make up the Frailes group plus the ridge coming down from Fraile Grande create a glacial basin where basecamp is placed. To reach the basin from Canónigo, cross the glacier and the ridge coming down from Fraile Grande and drop down.

Note: Much confusion surrounds the names and first ascents of the Fraile peaks.

Fraile Grande (5,180 m/16,990 ft) was first climbed via the northeast ridge on December 1, 1972, by Lorenzo Lorenzi, Armando Perron, and Marino Tremonti (Italy).

For the rest of the Frailes (Central, Oriental, and Beato, which lies on a spur coming off the main El Altar crescent), continue from Campamento El Sadday, cross the glacier, and continue to the rocky northwest ridge descending from Fraile Grande. Cross the ridge and drop down to camp in the cirque formed by the three remaining Fraile peaks.

sangay (sangai)

5,230 m/17,160 ft

AUGUST 4, 1929, WADDELL AUSTIN, ROBERT MOORE, TERRIS MOORE, AND

LEWIS THORNE (U.S.)

Maps: Llactapampa de Alao, Volcán Sangay

Sangay is the most continuously active volcano in the world and the most hardcore mountain in Ecuador to climb because of the demanding nature of the approach and the prevailing appalling weather. As Michael Koerner wrote: "Sangay means 'hell.' Getting there is the reason why . . . if you want to watch the sky glow at night and dodge flaming boulders the size of houses by day, this is the trip for you" (*Fool's Climbing Guide*, 1976).

Different interpretations for the name of the mountain exist. Some say it is from the Quichua word *samkay,* meaning "to frighten, scare, or terrorize"; others, primarily people living in the east, say it is from the word *shanga,* meaning "good-natured." The reason for this wide disparity is that despite Sangay's high level of activity, it has not damaged any of the surrounding areas.

Vulcanologists do not view the mountain as dangerous because the numerous eruptions (up to three per minute) prevent a big and dangerous build-up of gas that could cause a large eruption devastating a wide area. However, this does not prevent climbers from being killed by flying rocks—a helmet is essential.

The height of Sangay appears to vary depending on volcanic activity. Recorded heights range from 5,160 m/16,929 ft (Escuela Politécnica Nacional, 1975) to 5,323 m/17,463 ft (Bonington, 1966).

A summit bid needs a minimum of 7 days there and back from Quito and often 10 days, so plan accordingly. It took the first ascenders 28 days to find a way through to and then up the mountain.

During the mid-1990s Sangay quieted down and eruptions were confined, mainly, to emissions of gas, and rocks were not being thrown more

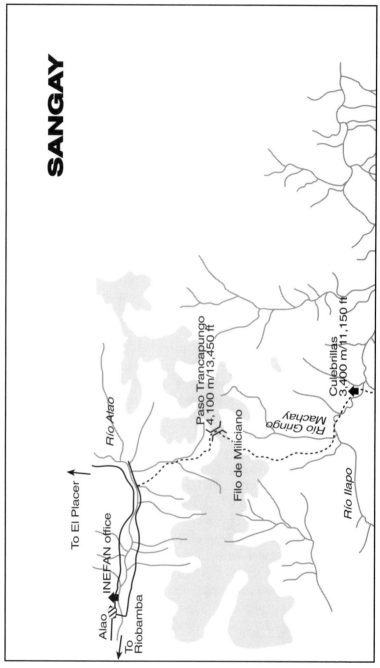

SANGAY

Rio Atao

To El Placer

INEFAN office

Alao

To Riobamba

Paso Trancapungo
4,100 m/13,450 ft

Filo de Miliciano

Rio Gringo
Machay

Culebrillas
3,400 m/11,150 ft

Rio Ilapo

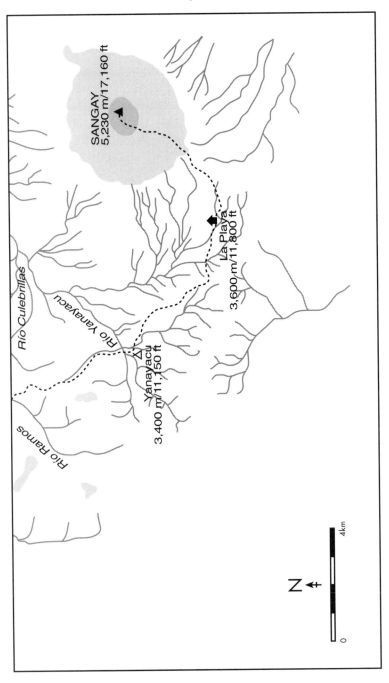

SANGAY
5,230 m/17,160 ft

La Playa
3,600 m/11,800 ft

Yanayacu
3,400 m/11,150 ft

Río Culebrillas

Río Yanayacu

Río Ramos

N

0   4km

A dry Sangay showing what's left of the glacier

than 50 m/165 ft from whichever crater was active. However, this situation could change at any time and rocks weighing as much as one ton and moving at 80 kmh/50 mph are not unusual. There are other factors to take into account: the rockfall danger is more serious when there is no snow on the mountain and in windy conditions when rocks get dislodged from the unstable slopes high on the mountain. In cloudy conditions you cannot see the falling rocks. Rain leads to a higher level of volcanic activity because the rainwater seeps down to the hot rock below and then gets vaporized. Helmets are essential, but ropes are not advisable because they restrict maneuverability in the event of a violent eruption. Clouds of sulfur gas have rendered people unconscious.

Rain. There is a lot of it in this area. Allegedly, the best time for Sangay is November to February, but the term "best" is relative. The 1929 first ascenders climbing in August were in continuous rain for 18 days; therefore, "best" can be taken to mean less than 18 days of continuous rain. In and immediately after heavy rainfall, streams become rivers and crossings become serious. On top of this, the streams/rivers become full of mud and so do not provide drinking water. After particularly heavy rainfall, landslides can also render the approach impossible. If it is raining hard on summit day, you face a high risk of hypothermia unless you have a complete set of dry clothes to change into at the glacier.

Now that the IGM has produced a map to the area, it is feasible to go in without a guide as long as your navigation skills are well honed. The trail is clear, if often muddy. However, the weather is predominantly bad with minimal visibility—a large percentage of people who have climbed Sangay appear not to have actually seen what they climbed. A guide from Alao will take you to the base of the glacier. No local climbed to the summit until 1989, and it is still not a popular route.

There are thirty-three guides in the San Antonio guides' association in Alao. Ask the park guardian at the INEFAN office for a guide, and he will put you in touch with one. A guide costs approximately US$8 per day (plus the park entrance fee of US$10), but this fee varies according to the size of the group—bigger groups get charged more. You must provide food and tent space for the guide. Guides will tell you it takes 3 days to reach the La Playa camp, but a fit group in reasonable condition can get there in 2 days, especially if you hire horses to carry the kit for the first day (US$8 per horse, each horse can carry three rucksacks). If you can get to Culebrillas in 1 day and all the way to La Playa in 1 day and back out in a similar fashion, then you do not need a tent. This is a gamble.

ACCESS

From Quito's Terminal Terrestre, take a bus to Riobamba (3½ hours, US$3). In Riobamba take a taxi (less than 10 minutes, US$1.10) to Parque La Libertad where there are buses to Alao most days until about 12:30 P.M. (The exception is Thursday when the last bus is around 8:00 A.M.) The drive time is 2 hours, but with loading, unloading, helping other buses in difficulty, flat tires, stand-offs with other vehicles on the narrow road, and so forth, you are unlikely to get away with less than 3 hours. However, the road is spectacular and well worth the journey that costs US$0.80.

Return buses to Riobamba leave Alao around 5:00 A.M. to get to Riobamba in time for market. There is also a milk truck at 8:00 A.M.

In Alao, walk up the road to the INEFAN office. If the guardian is not there, start asking for him. It costs US$0.80 to spend the night in the

INEFAN office, which has a kitchen, a bathroom, three beds, and plenty of floor space. It costs US$0.55 to camp outside. The park entrance fee is US$10.

Basics are available in Alao, but buy gas in Riobamba at the latest.

Jeep hire from Quito is US$160 for up to four people, US$40 for each additional person up to nine.

APPROACH

Day 1: Do not carry on up the road from the INEFAN office at 3,250 m/ 10,660 ft unless you want to add an extra river crossing to the day. Instead, walk back toward Riobamba for 15 minutes. When you get to the Casa de Comunidad and before you get to the Escuela Gonzalo Pizarro, look out for a path leading down left to a wooden footbridge across the Río Alao. Cross the bridge, go up the other side, turn left, and follow the road, which becomes a track.

After 1 hour the track runs next to the river where it is broad and can be forded. A path runs up right between two barbed-wire fences. At the top, turn left and a couple of minutes later after crossing a log-and-mud bridge, turn right and head up. After 1¼ hours you reach a flat clear section where camping is possible. Another 1¼ hours brings you to Paso Trancapungo at 4,100 m/13,450 ft and the park boundary, which is marked by a sign.

The approach to Sangay

A better, drier, flatter, wider path continues on the other side of the pass on the Filo de Miliciano, contouring and giving views of the flat Culebrillas valley and, allegedly, Sangay itself. After 45 minutes there is a flat spot with a stream (possible camping) and then the path starts to drop, bringing you to the Río Gringo Machay in 1½ hours. The path goes across the river, but 15 minutes later you have to recross it back to the other side. However, if you stay on the left side, you can pick a way around. Following the path or not you arrive at two wood and straw huts (*chozas*) in a field surrounded by a moat in 45 minutes from the first river crossing. This is Culebrillas, at 3,400 m/11,150 ft.

Day 2: On a good day you can see Sangay from Culebrillas lying to the southeast. However, the route goes south. With your back to the bigger of the two *chozas*, you can see a path on the other side of the Río Ilapo that becomes the Río Culebrillas. Ford the river and follow the path up on the other side; then drop down to a second river crossing (the Río Ramos) in 10 minutes. After another 10 minutes, the path runs along the bottom of a grassy field full of hoof holes. Leave the path and head up right through the field. At the top, the path reappears, and you begin an often steep and heavily vegetated climb to a small clearing on a ridge at 3,750 m/12,300 ft in 1¼ hours.

Warning: If you use the vegetation to pull up on, do not let your hand slip while grasping any of the plants—many of them are sharp enough to slice through your skin.

Turn left and follow the ridge for 10 minutes before dropping down. Then follow a stream down for 2 hours. This section involves multiple crossings before you get to a big crossing to reach a clearing with another stream coming down from the right. Head up on the right side to reach another clearing after 10 minutes. This is Yanayacu at 3,400 m/11,150 ft.

If you can reach Yanayacu around midday and the group is going well, you could continue to La Playa the same day. The advantage of this is that you don't have to camp at Yanayacu and can spend the night in the *choza* at La Playa. However, this is a long and hard day.

From Yanayacu, continue up the right side of the stream for a couple of minutes and then cross the stream and head up the side valley on the other side. After 45 minutes of ascent, you reach a ridge. Turn left and follow the ridge for 1½ hours until you reach a clearing at 3,800 m/ 12,470 ft. People sometimes choose to camp here, but there is no water. At the clearing, turn left, leave the main ridge, and follow a subsidiary

NORMAL ROUTE

SANGAY
FROM EL ALTAR TO THE NORTH

ridge down to reach a stream crossing in 30 minutes. Go up the side valley on the other side to reach a ridge, drop down to another stream crossing, go up the side valley on the other side to reach another ridge, and then go down again. Cross the river, turn right, and then follow the path up to reach a *choza*, which is in the area known as La Playa (the beach), 1 hour from the first stream crossing after the long ridge.

ALTERNATIVE APPROACHES

An alternative route from Alao to Culebrillas is via Hacienda Eten, south of Alao. Stay on the left bank of the river, heading south, before you head up left to a pass, drop down, cross the river, and then follow the right bank down to Culebrillas.

Sangay has been approached from Licto via Hacienda Guargalla, Plazapampa, and then on to Yanayacu.

From Macas, follow the Río Volcán upstream through the jungle. Take a machete and a sharpening stone. You will need both.

NORMAL ROUTE

La Playa is at 3,600 m/11,800 ft, leaving nearly 1,700 m/5,600 ft of ascent to the summit. In 1929 the first ascenders put in a high camp at the snow line at 4,500 m/14,760 ft. However, guides will tell you it is too dangerous to establish a high camp because of the possibility of rockfall. Although a summit push of 1,700 m/5,600 ft sounds horrendous, it is basically a walk and it is possible to do it in 7 hours. Just make sure you leave at 2 A.M.

With your back to the *choza*, turn right and follow the path to reach a river crossing after 15 minutes. Head up the valley and, when it forks, stay left. Twenty minutes later head up right, following the path that goes steeply up onto the ridge—if you reach a waterfall, you have missed the path and gone too far up the valley. After 30 minutes, drop down off the ridge and follow the path up the other side. After moving around the mountain, the path eventually goes up northeast toward the glacier on the north face in another 2½ hours. Either head straight up the glacier or stick to the scree slopes to reach the crater in 3 hours.

Descent: Same; 1 hour down the glacier, 2¼ hours back to La Playa. It is possible to get from La Playa to Culebrillas in one hard day, but you need to be in Yanayacu before 11 A.M. if you are going to try this.

Appendix A

MEDICAL KIT

Because access in Ecuador is so easy, there is no need to go overboard with a medical kit. Take the essentials, and you can get anything else you need when you get back to civilization, which never takes that long.

Note: Many but not all of the drugs below can be bought over the counter in pharmacies in Ecuador.

Altitude drugs

Acetazolamide—250mg pills or sustainable release tablets (for mountain sickness/acclimatization)

Nifedipine—10mg capsules (for High Altitude Pulmonary Edema)

Dexamethasone—pills and injectable version plus 5ml syringe and injection water (for High Altitude Cerebral Edema)

Painkillers

Paracetamol/aspirin (for headaches)

Ibuprofen (for sprains and muscle pain)

Temgesic/Demarol (for bone breaks)

Antibiotics

Ciprofloxacin (general and for persistent diarrhea)

Tinidazole (for giardiasis)

Doxycicline (general)

Other medications

Loperamide (to stop diarrhea when you must travel)

Amethocaine eye drops (for relief of pain, including snow blindness)

clove oil (for relief of tooth pain)

Bonjela (for relief of gum pain)

oral rehydration salts—available from pharmacists, ask for *sales de rehidratación oral* (for diarrhea)

Other items
space blanket
bandages and elastic bandages
suture strips
Band-Aids/plasters
Menolin pads
antiseptic cream
Micropore and zinc oxide tape
safety pins

Appendix B

EQUIPMENT

For the nontechnical hikes and scrambles (Chiles, Corazón, Guagua Pichincha, Imbabura, Mojanda, Rumiñahui Central and Sur), no technical climbing gear is necessary.

For the rubble tops (Cotacachi, Iliniza Norte in dry conditions, Rumiñahui Norte, and Sincholagua), you can get to within 50 m/165 ft of the summits without climbing. However, there are sections of rock climbing on bad rock. A helmet is essential, as well as a rope and sling to rappel on all but Iliniza Norte. Quilindaña is a technical rock climb needing a full selection of rock climbing protection.

For the longer and wetter approaches (Hermoso, Sangay, and Sara Urcu), dry bags are essential to protect your kit during possibly days of continuous rain. A tent with a separate flysheet and inner is advisable—the inner will be dry after use and can be kept that way in a dry bag. Trek wearing synthetic thermals and waterproofs—if you sleep in your thermals they will dry overnight. A synthetic sleeping bag is better than a down bag, which is not warm when wet. Some people advise rubber boots. These will keep your feet drier for longer and dry far more quickly than leather boots, which will get wet and will not dry during the trip. However, rubber boots provide little foot support and no ankle support, which is essential for this type of terrain. A good supply of foot-sized plastic bags will keep your feet warm inside your boots even when your boots are soaked. A machete is useful and makes finding the way back a lot easier, plus it helps keep the trail open. There are glaciers on Sangay and Sara Urcu, so you need crampons and an ice ax (plus a helmet for Sangay).

For the snow/ice climbs (the Big Ten, including Iliniza Norte in snowy/icy conditions and Tungurahua, but excluding Sangay), the full range of high altitude snow and ice climbing equipment and clothing is necessary. Two of the Big Ten, Carihuairazo and Iliniza Norte, also need rock climbing gear—a selection of pitons and slings plus spare cord and tape for rappels.

EQUIPMENT LIST (WITH ECUADORIAN SPANISH TRANSLATION)

Clothing
balaclava *(pasamontaña)*
thermal top and bottom *(ropa interior termica)*
fleece jacket *(chaqueta de pile)*
thin gloves *(guantes delgados)*
inner gloves *(guantes interiores)*
synthetic trousers *(pantalones sinteticas)*
thin synthetic socks *(calcetines delgados sinteticos)*
thick wool socks *(calcetines gruesos de lana)*
breathable waterproof jacket with integral hood *(chaqueta con capucha)*
breathable waterproof mitts *(mittones)*
breathable waterproof bibs *(salopettes/overol impermeable)*
gaiters *(polainas)*
plastic boots *(botas plasticas)*
anti–ball up plates *(antibotas)*
walking boots and socks *(botas de trekking)*

Sun protection
sunhat *(gorra)*
sun cream *(crema contra el sol)*
100-percent-UV-proof glacier glasses *(gafas con protección UV)*
100-percent-UV-proof ski goggles *(gafas de ski)*
lip salve *(crema para los labios)*
medical kit *(botiquín de primeros auxilios)*

Climbing supplies
80 liter+ rucksack *(mochila)*
helmet *(casco)*
headlamp that runs on a flat-type battery, and spare battery (other batteries go dead very quickly at altitude) *(linterna frontal y pila de repuesto)*
harness *(arnés)*
12-point crampons *(crampones de 12 puntas)*

ice ax and hammer *(piolet y martillo)*
screwgate and normal carabiners *(mosquetones de seguridad y normales)*
slings *(cintas)*
ice screws *(tornillos de hielo)*
snow stakes *(estacas de nieve)*
pitons *(pitones)*
50 m x 9 mm rope *(cuerda)*
cord/tape for rappels *(cordino/cinta para rapel)*
prussik loops *(nudos prussik)*
pulley *(polea)*

Camping supplies

down sleeping bag *(saco de dormir de pluma)*
sleeping bag liner *(saco de dormir interno)*
sleeping mat *(aislante)*
tent *(carpa)*
snow pegs *(clavos para nieve)*
stove and fuel *(cocineta y combustible)*
lighters *(encendedores)*
pans, mug, spoon *(ollas, taza, cuchara)*
food *(comida)*
iodine tincture *(yodo)*
1 l/qt water bottle *(cantimplora)*
4 l/qt water bag *(bolsa de agua de 4 litros)*
penknife *(navaja)*
duct tape *(cinta de embalaje)*

Miscellaneous

map *(mapa)*
compass *(brújula)*
whistle *(pito)*
money (in S/10,000 denomination notes) *(dinero)*
passport (legal requirement) *(pasaporte)*
camera, spare batteries, and spare film *(cámara fotográfica, pilas de repuesto, pelicula)*
notebook, ballpoint pen, and pencil *(libreta, bolígrafo, lapiz)*

Optional

neoprene facemask *(máscara de neopreno)*
fleece trousers *(antalones de pile)*
down jacket *(chaqueta de pluma)*

For longer trips add the following:

sewing kit *(kit de costura)*
extra fuel bottle *(botella de combustible extra)*
spare pick *(punta de piolet de repuesto)*
second rucksack *(segunda mochila)*
book *(libro)*
Vitamin C and iron tablets *(tabletas de vitamina C y hierro)*
waterproof stuff sacks *(bolsas impermeables)*
spare laces, gloves, and mitts *(cordones, guantes, y mittones extras)*
toothbrush and paste, soap, comb *(cepillo y pasta de dientes, jabón, peine)*

Appendix C

FURTHER READING

Mountaineering guidebooks

Cruz, Marco. *Die Schneeberge Ecuadors*. Naila: Frank Verlag, 1983. (German) Beautiful photographs, excellent topos, and good approach maps to thirty of Ecuador's mountains. A bit dated, but the major problem is that it's in German.

Koerner, Michael. *The Fool's Climbing Guide to Ecuador and Peru: A Work of Fiction and Plagiarism*. Colorado: Buzzard Mountaineering, 1976. Concise and funny more than practical because of its age, but a very enjoyable read.

Landazuri, Freddy, Ivan Rojas, and Marcos Serrano. *Montañas del Sol*. Quito: Campo Abierto, 1994. (Spanish) A good climbing guidebook to twenty-six mountains in Ecuador, but it lacks topo diagrams and public transport information.

Rachowiecki, Rob, and Mark Thurber. *Climbing and Hiking in Ecuador*. 4th ed. Chalfont St Peter: Bradt, 1997. Gets better every edition, covers a number of treks and sub-5,000-m/16,000-ft peaks suitable for acclimatizing as well as descriptions of routes on the Big Ten.

Mountaineering

Anhalzer, Jorge. *Andes*. Quito: 1997. (Spanglish) A beautiful, softcover coffee-table book.

Bonington, Chris. *The Next Horizon*. London: Gollancz, 1973. Includes the British mountaineer's 9-day machete trip from Macas to Sangay and the return trip in from Alao.

Cruz, Marco. *Montañas del Ecuador*. Quito: Dinediciones, 1993. (Spanish) A beautiful coffee-table book full of color photographs taken by Ecuador's leading guide of the last thirty years.

Francou, Bernard, and Patrick Wagnon. *Cordillères andines*. Grenoble: Glénat, 1998. (French) Beautiful and informative about many aspects of the Andes in Ecuador, Peru, and Bolivia. Written and photographed by two leading French glaciologists.

MacInnes, Hamish. *Beyond the Ranges: Five Years in the Life of Hamish MacInnes.* London: Gollancz, 1984. Includes the Scottish mountaineer's three trips to the Llanganates in search of Inca treasure with Joe Brown and Yvon Chouinard.

Snailham, Richard. *Sangay Survived.* London: Hutchinson, 1978. The account of the 1976 six-man British expedition that left two dead and three seriously injured.

Whymper, Edward. *Travels Amongst the Great Andes of the Equator.* London: Murray, 1892, reprinted. Absolute classic, one of the best books written about climbing anything, anywhere (especially if you ignore any paragraph discussing the differences between the mercurial and aneroid barometers).

Vulcanology

Hall, Dr. Minard. *El Volcanismo en el Ecuador.* Quito: IPGH, 1977. (Spanish) Detailed descriptions of all the important volcanoes in the country.

Mothes, Patricia, ed. *El Paisaje: Volcánico de la Sierra Ecuatoriana.* Quito: Corporación Editora Nacional, 1991. (Spanish) The most modern work on the subject.

Medical

Forgey, William, M.D., ed. *Practice Guidelines for Wilderness Emergency Care.* Indiana: I.C.S. Books Inc., 1995. A concise and very readable wilderness medical guide that includes specific chapters on high altitude illness, hypothermia, and frostbite as well as other sorts of illnesses and injuries possible in the outdoors.

Pollard, Andrew, and David Murdoch. *The High Altitude Medicine Handbook.* Oxford and New York: Radcliffe, 1997. Written by two climbing doctors, this concise book covers everything you need to know about altitude medicine in a detailed but readable way. Excellent.

Steele, Peter. *Medical Handbook for Mountaineers.* London: Constable, 1988. First aid on the mountain: airway, breathing, circulation, patching people up, and getting them off the hill.

Wilkerson, James, M.D., ed. *Medicine for Mountaineering,* 4th ed. Seattle: The Mountaineers, 1997. Without doubt, the most comprehensive book on mountain medicine, but worth reading before you go on a trip—it's over 400 pages long.

General

Box, Ben, ed. *South American Handbook*. Bath: Footprint, annual. Most up-to-date general guidebook—revised every year—covering the whole of the continent.

Kunstaetter, Robert and Daisy. *Latin American Travel Advisor*. Quito: LATA, quarterly. News bulletin providing up-to-date information on travel in Ecuador and sixteen other Latin American countries. Contact LATA, P.O. Box 17-17-908, Quito, Ecuador, *lata@pi.pro.ec*

Murphy, Alan, ed. *Ecuador Handbook*. 2nd ed. Bath: Footprint, 1999 and every two years thereafter. The most up-to-date, detailed, general guide to the country—where to stay, where to eat, and how to get there.

Rachowiecki, Rob. *Ecuador Travel Survival Kit*. 5th ed. Australia: Lonely Planet, 2000. The most detailed general guide to the country.

Roos, Wilma, and Omer van Renterghem. *Ecuador in Focus*. London: Latin American Bureau, 1997. Clear, concise roundup of politics, economics, history, and culture. Excellent.

Index

Page numbers in **boldface** denote topos; those in *italics* denote maps.

accidents 51
acclimatization 36–38
acetalozamide 37, 178
agencies 42–43
altitude sickness 38, 47–49, 178–179
Antisana 112–114, *113*
  Máxima *113*, 115–118, **116–117**
  Nor-Oriental *113*, 118–120, *119*
  Oriental *113*, 120, **121**
  Pico Sur *113*, 122–124, **123**
  traverse 124
Azul, Laguna *159*

bases 35
birds 31
Bonington, Chris 20

camping supplies 181–182
Canónigo *156*, 157, *159*, 167
Carihuairazo 84, 85, **88**
  Máxima 84, 85, *87*
Carrels, Louis 18
Cayambe 23, 99, *100–101*, 102–103, **104, 106**
  Máxima *100*, 103, 105
  Pico Nor-Este *100*, 107
Cerro Negro *61*, 67–69

Chiles 55–59, *56*, **57**
Chimborazo 84, 89–90, 90, **92**
  Nicolás Martínez *86*, 94–95
  Politécnica *86*, 94
  traverses 95
  Veintemilla *86*, 89
  Whymper *86*, 90, 93–94
climbing history 15–22
climbing supplies 181–182
clothing 181
Cordillera Occidental 12, 15
Cordillera Oriental 15
Cotacachi 60–64, *61*, **62**
Cotopaxi 16–17, 136–140, **139**
Cubre Máxima *see* Máxima
Cuicocha 24
Cumbre Nor-Oriental *see* Nor-Oriental
Cumbre Oriental *see* Oriental
Cumbre Politécnica *see* Politécnica
Cumbre Veintemilla *see* Veintemilla
Cumbre Whymper *see* Whymper
currency 36

dexamethasone 49

Ecuadorian climbers 21–22
El Altar 20, 155–161, *156, 158–159*
  northern peaks:
  Canónigo *156,* 157, *159,* 167
  Frailes *156,* 167–168
  southern peaks:
  Monja Chica *156,* 164, 166
  Monja Grande *156,* 164, **165**
  Obispo *156,* 157, *159,* 161–164,
  162
environmental impact 52
equipment 40, 180–183

flora 32–33
food 39
food poisoning 50
Frailes *156,* 167–168
fuel 39
Fuya Fuya *61,* 65, 67

geology 22–27
giardiasis 50
glaciers 27–29
Guagua Pinchincha 70–73, *71*
guides 44

health considerations
  accidents 51
  acclimatization 36–38
  acetalozamide 37, 178
  altitude sickness 38, 47–49,
  178–179
  food 39
  food poisoning 50
  high altitude cerebral edema
  (HACE) 48–49
  high altitude pulmonary
  edema (HAPE) 48

  medical kit 178–179
  medications 178–179
  rescues 51
  safety 11
  sleep disturbances 49
  sun protection 49–50, 181
  water 50
Hermoso 144–149, *145,* **148**
high altitude cerebral edema
  (HACE) 48–49
high altitude pulmonary edema
  (HAPE) 48
history 15–22
huts 45–46

Iliniza Norte 75, 77–79, **78**
Ilinizas 74–77
  Norte 75, 77–79, **78**
  Sur 75, 79–83, **80**
Iliniza Sur 75, **76,** 79–83, **80**
Imbabura *96,* 96–98
Integral 95
Interandean region 12, 15

Lago San Pablo 96
lahars 25
lodging 45–46

mammals 29–30
Mandur, Laguna *159*
maps
  Ecuador *13–14*
  key to 6
  where to buy 47
Martínez, Nicolás 18–19, 21–22
Máxima
  Antisana *113,* 115–118, **116–**
  117

Carihuairazo 84–85, *87*
Cayambe *100,* 103, 105
medical kit 178–179
medications 178–179
Mojanda *61*
    Cerro Negro *61,* 67–69
    description of 65
    Fuya Fuya *61,* 65, 67
Monja Chica *156,* 164, 166
Monja Grande *156,* 164, **165**
Moore, Robert 19–20

natural history 29–33
Negra, Laguna *159*
Nor-Oriental *113,* 118–120, **119**

Obispo *156,* 157, *159,* 161–164,
    162
Oriental *113,* 120, **121**

Padre Encantado *71*
parks 45
passport 36
peaks 14
photography 40
Pico Nor-Este *100,* 107
Pico Sur *113,* 122–124, **123**
Politécnica *86,* 94
Pululahua 24

Quilindaña 141–143, **142**
Quito 34

rescues 51
Rucu Pinchincha *71*
Rumiñahui 131
    Central *126,* 131–133, **132**
    Norte *126,* 131–133, **132**

Sur *126,* **132,** 134–135

safety 11
Sangay 19, 169–177, *170–171,* **176**
Sara Urcu *101,* 108–111, **110**
seasons 41–42
security 46–47
Sincholagua 125–130, *126–127,*
    129
sleep disturbances 49
snow blindness 50
South American Explorers' Club
    43–44
Spanish 38–39
stratovolcanoes 23
sun protection 49–50, 181
supplies 181–183

Tambo, Laguna *145*
transportation 44–45
Tungurahua 150–154, *151,* **153**

Veintemilla *86*
Verde, Laguna *159*
visa 36
volcanoes 15, 22–27

water 50
Whymper *86,* 90, 93–94
Whymper, Edward 16–18, 27

Yanacocha, Laguna *145*
Yurac Ilanganati *see* Hermoso

About the Author

Yossi Brain
1967–1999

Yossi Brain topping out on the 1,000 m/3,300 ft west face of Huayna Potosí
(Photo by Gerry Arcari)

While recovering in the intensive care unit of Chamonix hospital following a rather rapid descent of the 800 m/2,600 ft northeast face of Les
Courtes in the French Alps in 1994, Yossi Brain decided to quit his job
as a political reporter for an evening newspaper in Britain and take up
climbing full time. He intended to return to Ecuador, where he first

climbed in 1990, but he ended up in Bolivia guiding mountaineering trips from La Paz. Over the years, he found his way back to Ecuador as an escape from the Bolivian wet season. In September 1999, Yossi was caught in an avalanche and lost his life while doing what he loved most.

Yossi was a member of the American Alpine Club, the South American Explorers' Club, and the Asociación de Guias de Montaña de Bolivia. He was a contributor to the *American Alpine Journal, Alpine Journal,* and *High Magazine Mountain Info,* and he was the resident Bolivia correspondent for the *South American Handbook* and a contributor to the guide for Ecuador. Yossi's other books published by The Mountaineers include *Bolivia: A Climbing Guide* (1999) and *Trekking in Bolivia* (1997).

Yossi's meticulous research both in the library and on the mountains, brought together with his own special brand of humor, make this an unsurpassed guide for Ecuadorian mountaineering. Yossi Brain was an example to us all. He worked hard and played hard, packing several successful careers into 32 years. He was a legend in his own lifetime in Bolivia and will be sadly missed in the mountains of South America.

THE MOUNTAINEERS, founded in 1906, is a nonprofit outdoor activity and conservation club, whose mission is "to explore, study, preserve, and enjoy the natural beauty of the outdoors. . . . " Based in Seattle, Washington, the club is now the third-largest such organization in the United States, with 15,000 members and five branches throughout Washington State.

The Mountaineers sponsors both classes and year-round outdoor activities in the Pacific Northwest, which include hiking, mountain climbing, ski-touring, snowshoeing, bicycling, camping, kayaking and canoeing, nature study, sailing, and adventure travel. The club's conservation division supports environmental causes through educational activities, sponsoring legislation, and presenting informational programs. All club activities are led by skilled, experienced volunteers, who are dedicated to promoting safe and responsible enjoyment and preservation of the outdoors.

If you would like to participate in these organized outdoor activities or the club's programs, consider a membership in The Mountaineers. For information and an application, write or call The Mountaineers, Club Headquarters, 300 Third Avenue West, Seattle, Washington 98119; 206-284-6310.

The Mountaineers Books, an active, nonprofit publishing program of the club, produces guidebooks, instructional texts, historical works, natural history guides, and works on environmental conservation. All books produced by The Mountaineers fulfill the club's mission.

Send or call for our catalog of more than 450 outdoor titles:

The Mountaineers Books
1001 SW Klickitat Way, Suite 201
Seattle, WA 98134
800-553-4453
mbooks@mountaineers.org
www.mountaineersbooks.org